THE ISIS GENOCIDE DECLARATION: WHAT NEXT?

HEARING

BEFORE THE

SUBCOMMITTEE ON AFRICA, GLOBAL HEALTH, GLOBAL HUMAN RIGHTS, AND INTERNATIONAL ORGANIZATIONS

OF THE

COMMITTEE ON FOREIGN AFFAIRS
HOUSE OF REPRESENTATIVES

ONE HUNDRED FOURTEENTH CONGRESS

SECOND SESSION

MAY 26, 2016

Serial No. 114–211

Printed for the use of the Committee on Foreign Affairs

Available via the World Wide Web: http://www.foreignaffairs.house.gov/ or http://www.gpo.gov/fdsys/

U.S. GOVERNMENT PUBLISHING OFFICE

20–260PDF   WASHINGTON : 2016

For sale by the Superintendent of Documents, U.S. Government Publishing Office
Internet: bookstore.gpo.gov   Phone: toll free (866) 512–1800; DC area (202) 512–1800
Fax: (202) 512–2104   Mail: Stop IDCC, Washington, DC 20402–0001

COMMITTEE ON FOREIGN AFFAIRS

EDWARD R. ROYCE, California, *Chairman*

CHRISTOPHER H. SMITH, New Jersey
ILEANA ROS-LEHTINEN, Florida
DANA ROHRABACHER, California
STEVE CHABOT, Ohio
JOE WILSON, South Carolina
MICHAEL T. McCAUL, Texas
TED POE, Texas
MATT SALMON, Arizona
DARRELL E. ISSA, California
TOM MARINO, Pennsylvania
JEFF DUNCAN, South Carolina
MO BROOKS, Alabama
PAUL COOK, California
RANDY K. WEBER SR., Texas
SCOTT PERRY, Pennsylvania
RON DeSANTIS, Florida
MARK MEADOWS, North Carolina
TED S. YOHO, Florida
CURT CLAWSON, Florida
SCOTT DesJARLAIS, Tennessee
REID J. RIBBLE, Wisconsin
DAVID A. TROTT, Michigan
LEE M. ZELDIN, New York
DANIEL DONOVAN, New York

ELIOT L. ENGEL, New York
BRAD SHERMAN, California
GREGORY W. MEEKS, New York
ALBIO SIRES, New Jersey
GERALD E. CONNOLLY, Virginia
THEODORE E. DEUTCH, Florida
BRIAN HIGGINS, New York
KAREN BASS, California
WILLIAM KEATING, Massachusetts
DAVID CICILLINE, Rhode Island
ALAN GRAYSON, Florida
AMI BERA, California
ALAN S. LOWENTHAL, California
GRACE MENG, New York
LOIS FRANKEL, Florida
TULSI GABBARD, Hawaii
JOAQUIN CASTRO, Texas
ROBIN L. KELLY, Illinois
BRENDAN F. BOYLE, Pennsylvania

AMY PORTER, *Chief of Staff*   THOMAS SHEEHY, *Staff Director*
JASON STEINBAUM, *Democratic Staff Director*

———

SUBCOMMITTEE ON AFRICA, GLOBAL HEALTH, GLOBAL HUMAN RIGHTS, AND INTERNATIONAL ORGANIZATIONS

CHRISTOPHER H. SMITH, New Jersey, *Chairman*

MARK MEADOWS, North Carolina
CURT CLAWSON, Florida
SCOTT DesJARLAIS, Tennessee
DANIEL DONOVAN, New York

KAREN BASS, California
DAVID CICILLINE, Rhode Island
AMI BERA, California

CONTENTS

THE ISIS GENOCIDE DECLARATION: WHAT NEXT?

THURSDAY, MAY 26, 2016

House of Representatives,
Subcommittee on Africa, Global Health,
Global Human Rights, and International Organizations,
Committee on Foreign Affairs,
Washington, DC.

The subcommittee met, pursuant to notice, at 12:02 p.m., in room 2172, Rayburn House Office Building, Hon. Christopher H. Smith (chairman of the subcommittee) presiding.

Mr. SMITH. The subcommittee will come to order, and good afternoon and welcome to everyone. In January 2014, ISIS terrorists captured the city of Fallujah in central Iraq a decade after it had been won at the cost of so much American, Iraqi, and British blood. ISIS moved north, taking more territory, and conducting its genocidal campaign again Christians, Yazidis, and other religious minorities. By early August, Yazidi men, women, and children were trapped on Mount Sinjar facing annihilation when the U.S. initiated airstrikes to save them.

However, beyond that, it soon became clear that the administration had no comprehensive plan to prevent ISIS from continuing to commit genocide, mass atrocities, and war crimes or to roll ISIS back.

This subcommittee, along with the Middle East and North Africa Subcommittee, co-chaired by my good friend and colleague, Ileana Ros-Lehtinen, convened a hearing on the genocide in December 2014 and called for the administration to act before those communities of Christians and others were annihilated.

Meanwhile, across the porous border in Syria, the Assad regime was targeting and killing tens of thousands of civilians. I renewed my call again for a Syrian war crimes tribunal to be established to hold all sides in the conflict of Syria accountable, and we had heard from such great leaders, the former chief prosecutor who will testify today, David Crane, about the importance of taking action in a tribunal that had the flexibility and the capability to really hold people to account on all sides. The world knew that ISIS was committing genocide. Civil society groups, including some present at this hearing today, mobilized, writing letters and holding meetings with the administration, making statements and reporting stories.

As a matter of fact, parenthetically, my first hearing that I held here in this room was more than 3 years ago on the genocide against Christians. Why was there such an indifference on the part of some within the administration?

However, some members of the administration were pushing hard internally for the word ''genocide'' to be publicly spoken and for action to be swiftly taken. Yet the administration still had not acknowledged it and still had no strategy to prevent it from happening. Such was the situation in December 2015 when this subcommittee convened yet another hearing. Shortly after, the Congress passed and the President signed into law the Fiscal Year 2016 appropriations bill, the omnibus bill, which required the Secretary of State to report to Congress with his evaluation on whether ISIS had perpetrated genocide.

Perhaps the most important push outside the government and off the Hill was the 280-page report commissioned by the Knights of Columbus and developed in partnership with the tireless organization In Defense of Christians meticulously documenting the genocide against Christians. That report may have made the difference with the administration, so I am personally grateful to Carl Anderson, the Supreme Knight who is here to testify again, and for the Knights, along with the other groups, including A Demand For Action, that have done so much to ensure that genocide against Christians and others could not be ignored, trivialized, or denied.

The House passed H. Con. Res. 75, authored by my good friend and colleague, Jeff Fortenberry, together with the Syrian War Crimes Tribunal Resolution that I had sponsored, H. Con. Res. 121, 3 days before the Secretary's evaluation was due. Finally, on March 17, Secretary Kerry declared that ISIS is ''responsible for genocide against groups in areas under its control, including Yazidis, Christians, and Shia Muslims.''

Although the administration made the right determination, a long time coming but they did, the question arises now, now what? I already have concerns that historical mistakes are being repeated. Leading up to Secretary of State Colin Powell's historic genocide determination in September 2004—and I was very much a part of pushing for that to happen, along with others like Frank Wolf—the State Department's legal adviser had issued a memorandum that concluded that ''a determination that genocide has occurred in Darfur would have no immediate legal—as opposed to moral, political, or policy—consequences for the United States.''

Secretary Kerry's legal advisers reportedly reached the same conclusion before he made his determination about ISIS. And so it again begs the question, now what?

For years, the administration has been unwilling to effectively address the slaughters in Syria and Iraq. If it still thinks it has no obligation to act, it will likely continue its policy of acting too little too late. I am also concerned that the administration continues to conflate its strategy to combat ISIS with a strategy to protect religious minorities from genocide, war crimes, and mass atrocities. They are not the same. Combatting and defeating ISIS and Islamist extremism, of course, is essential. However, there are many other elements of an effective comprehensive civilian protection strategy, putting effective monitoring and response systems in place, and we have yet to hear them from the administration.

Civilian protection has long been missing from the administration's response to the carnage in Syria. More than half its population, an estimated 13.5 million inside Syria, as of May 2016, plus another 4.8 million registered as refugees abroad, are in need of humanitarian assistance and protection. According to an April 2016 review of the casualty estimates of that conflict, the number of people who have died during Syria's civil war conflict since March 11, 2011, range from 250,000 to 470,000. Notwithstanding the challenges of knowing exactly how many of those people were civilians and exactly how many were killed by the Assad regime and its proxies, we know this: The dictatorship has consistently, deliberately targeted civilians, hospitals, and schools with bombs and bullets and starved entire cities.

While Russia, Iran, and Hezbollah have fueled the fires of death in Syria, the administration has mostly just watched Syria burn. Let me also point out that, in his testimony today—and it is worth really highlighting because others will make similar points—but Carl Anderson makes the point that ''we are reliably informed that official government and U.N. aid does not reach the Christian genocide survivors in Iraq or in Syria. Repeatedly,'' he goes on to say, ''we hear from church leaders in the region that Christians and other genocide survivors are last in line for assistance from governments. Significantly, the Archdiocese of Erbil, where most Iraqi Christians now live, receives no money from any government whatsoever. If assistance from outside church-affiliated agencies ends in Erbil, Christians there will face a catastrophic humanitarian tragedy within 30 days. The situation is similar in Syria, according to Christian leaders there.''

There is no easy single solution to the threats to religious and ethnic minorities and other civilians in Iraq and Syria. Obstacles clearly abound, including failures to implement the Iraq Constitution, especially the decentralized power and localized governance and security; longstanding unresolved disputes between Iraqi Arabs and Kurds over territory and natural resources; lack of accountability for genocide, mass atrocities, war crimes, torture, kidnappings, displacement, and more by a range of actors; the actions of an indigenously developed, internally supported national reconciliation process; conflicts over revenue sharing, corruption and radicalization.

The list is long, complex, and it must never, however, be an excuse for indifference and inaction. However, unless key issues that preceded the genocide are addressed, the genocide may be perpetuated again, and it certainly is going on right now.

Over the coming weeks, I plan to introduce a comprehensive piece of legislation aimed at contributing to the safety and security of religious and ethnic minorities and civilians more broadly in Iraq and Syria. It will also address the need for accountability for genocide, mass atrocities in those conflicts, and will also again call for a tribunal, like we saw in Sierra Leone, Rwanda, or the former Yugoslavia, and I do hope that the Senate at some point, hopefully soon, takes up our resolution that is pending before the Senate Committee on Foreign Relations.

I would like to yield to my good friend and colleague, the ranking member, Ms. Bass.

4

Ms. BASS. Thank you, Mr. Chairman.

Good afternoon to the witnesses.

I look forward to hearing your perspectives regarding these critical issues. As you know, on March 17, 2016, Secretary of State John Kerry declared that ISIS is responsible for genocide against groups in areas under its control, including the Yazidis, Christians, and Shia Muslims. The Secretary went on to chronicle numerous atrocities against various ethnic and religious groups by ISIL over the last few years. The question posed to the witnesses today is a logical result of the determination of genocide, specifically what actions need to be taken by the U.S., the international community, and, frankly, the region, to prevent further genocide.

Secretary Kerry noted in his statement on March 17 that the best response to genocide is a reaffirmation of the fundamental right to survive of every grouped targeted for destruction.

I look forward to hearing from the witnesses today on how that can best be achieved, bearing in mind the ongoing suffering of women, men, and children who live in constant fear.

Thank you, Mr. Chairman.

Mr. SMITH. Thank you so much.

We are joined by the famous chairman, Dana Rohrabacher, the gentleman from California.

Mr. ROHRABACHER. Thank you very much, Mr. Chairman. When we come to this issue and we look at this, it behooves us to open our hearts and try to come up with a formula that is going to help those people who are who are most in need and people whose lives are most in jeopardy. And, unfortunately—and I am just going to have to say, and I will try not to make this political—but our President has not come to the standard that I believe is adequate to deal with this horrible situation and the challenge that we face in the Middle East. It could be the guy's unable to say ''radical Islamic terrorism,'' even after our Ambassador was slaughtered and murdered in Benghazi, and he hasn't been able to say those words since.

And we have been on him because of that, but that mindset will have implications, and it has implications in the issues that we are talking today. We have innocent people by the hundreds of thousands, if not by the millions, who are in jeopardy of being slaughtered in the same way the Jews were slaughtered during the Holocaust.

And when I look at the figures of the people who are being permitted into this country right now under this administration, the Christians who are the basic target, the most vocalized target of these radical Muslims who are there who are involved with this terrorist activity, the Christians are underrepresented in the number of immigrants in terms of refugees and in terms of people who are actually immigrating from those countries in which they have been targeted for genocide. This is wrong. This is absolutely wrong. It is like sending the Jews back and saying: We are going to have a more open policy because of the Nazis, but the Jews aren't going to be able to come in.

I would hope that we as Americans, both Republicans, Democrats, and this administration and this Congress, recognize we are in a moment now where we are defining ourselves, and we need to make sure that when Christians are under the threat of genocide, that they should have some priority over those other people in those countries that are not targets of genocide. And this isn't some sort of discrimination against Muslims or anybody else or Shiites or anybody else, but let's recognize that that is what is going on and that is what the threat is and deal with the threat and not try to have a debate that is sanitized over here in theory.

So I am very pleased, and I am grateful to Congressman Smith, who, again, has demonstrated his total commitment to human rights of every person on this planet and how he commits himself to these issues.

Chairman Smith, I would suggest that we again, and today we are reaffirming that we hear ISIL when they say that they are going to slaughter all the Christians. We hear them when they make proclamations of genocide against Christians and, yes, Yazidis as well and others as well, but specifically to the Christians and the Yazidis, and that we will then make sure that we mobilize, and we help mobilize the American people, which is what this hearing is all about, to save the Christians from genocide. It is up to us. I don't want future generations to look back on this generation of Americans and say: They closed their ears because they had clinical analysis to do whether or not you could single out one group that is being targeted for genocide for preferential treatment in terms of immigration and refugee status. I don't want to hear that, which resulted in hundreds of thousands or maybe millions of Christians dying in the Middle East.

Let's get serious about this. I appreciate this opportunity to join you, Mr. Chairman, in this very moral effort to make sure our country is practical and is courageous enough to handle this challenge, this moral challenge of our day, to save the people who are being targeted for genocide. Thank you very much.

Mr. SMITH. Thank you, Chairman Rohrabacher, for your very powerful statement and for your leadership on human rights. I appreciate it. We all do.

I would like to introduce our very distinguished panel beginning with Mr. Carl Anderson, who is Supreme Knight of the Knights of Columbus, where he is chief executive officer and chairman of the board of the world's largest Catholic family fraternal service organization, with over 1.9 million members. Mr. Anderson has had a distinguished career in public service and as an educator as well. From 1983 to 1987, he served in various positions in the Executive Office of the President of the United States, including Special Assistant to the President, and Acting Director of the White House Office of Public Liaison. Following his service in the House, he also served for nearly a decade as a member of the U.S. Commission on Civil Rights.

I will then move on to Mr. Sarhang Hamasaeed, who is a senior program officer for the Middle East and North Africa Programs at the U.S. Institute of Peace. He joined USIP in February 2011. He works on program management, organizational development, monitoring, and evaluation. He also provides political and policy analysis on Iraq to the Institute of Peace and other peacekeeping actors. As Deputy Director General of the Council of Ministers of the Kurdistan Regional Government of Iraq, he managed strategic government modernization initiatives through information technology with the goal of helping to improve governance and service delivery. He has also worked with the Research Triangle Institute International, Kurdistan Save the Children, the Los Angeles Times, and other media organizations.

We will then hear from Mr. Johnny Oram who is the executive director of the Chaldean Assyrian Business Alliance, dedicated to professional and social advancement of communities worldwide. He has been involved in the advocacy for the plight of the Iraqi and Syrian Christians who have been displaced due to the conflict. Additionally, Mr. Oram is involved in advocacy of the rights of the disabled, specifically those with autism spectrum disorder, or ASD. He has served in numerous capacities at the local, State, and Federal levels of government, worked for the Michigan legislature, Hawaii legislature, and in the U.S. Senate.

We will then hear from Ms. Naomi Kikoler, who is the Deputy Director of the Simon-Skjodt Center for the Prevention of Genocide at the United States Holocaust Museum. For 6 years, she developed and implemented the Global Centre for the Responsibility to Protect work on populations at risk and efforts to advance R2P globally and led the Center's advocacy, including targeting the U.N. Security Council. She is also an adjunct professor at the New School University and author of numerous publications previously. She worked on national security and refugee policy for Amnesty International Canada and in the office of the prosecutor of the United Nations International Criminal Tribunal for Rwanda.

We will then hear from Mr. David Crane, who was appointed a Professor of Practice at Syracuse University College of Law in December 2006. He was the founding chief prosecutor of the Special Court for Sierra Leone, an international war crimes tribunal that put many of the worst actors in that terrible, terrible tragedy behind bars. Ultimately, Charles Taylor got 50 years of prison sentence at The Hague because of the great landmark work that Professor Crane did. Professor Crane's mandate was to prosecute those who bore the greatest responsibility committed during the civil war in Sierra Leone in the 1990s. He served for more than 30 years in the Federal Government. He has held numerous key managerial positions and has been dogged in his work to document the atrocities that are occurring in Syria and in the region.

So thank you all for being here. What you convey to us and, by extension, to the Congress, hopefully to the administration, will help provide us with a roadmap going forward. So, Mr. Anderson, please proceed.

STATEMENT OF MR. CARL A. ANDERSON, SUPREME KNIGHT, KNIGHTS OF COLUMBUS

Mr. ANDERSON. Well, thank you very much, Mr. Chairman, for the opportunity to appear before the subcommittee today. The House of Representatives, the State Department, and the United States Commission on International Religious Freedom are all to be commended for declaring the situation confronting Christians and other religious minorities in the Middle East to be genocide. As we all know, the world's greatest humanitarian crisis since World War II is unfolding now in the Middle East. In addition to millions of refugees, many of the region's indigenous communities now face extinction. These communities may disappear in less than a decade, but their fate is not inevitable. The United States can avert this unfolding tragedy with a policy that contains, we believe, the following six principles: First, increase aid and ensure that it actually reaches those most in need. We are reliably informed, as the chairman has stated earlier, that official government and U.N. aid does not reach the Christian genocide survivors in Iraq and Syria. Repeatedly we hear from church leaders in the region that Christians and other genocide survivors are last in line for assistance from governments. Significantly the Archdiocese of Erbil, where most Iraqi Christians now live, receives no money from any government whatsoever. If assistance from outside church-affiliated agencies ends in Erbil, Christians there will face a catastrophic humanitarian tragedy within 30 days. And the situation is similar in Syria, according to Christian leaders there.

Those who face genocide are a tiny fraction of the population. They often must avoid official refugee camps because they are targeted for violence there by extremists. As a result, these minorities often do not get official aid, and this will continue to be the reality, unless specific action is taken to bring the aid to where these minorities are forced to reside by continuing violence.

Knights of Columbus and other private sources have responded to this situation, but nongovernmental organizations can only do so much. It is essential, therefore, that government aid is increased and that we ensure it reaches those most in need, even if special emergency appropriations are required to do this.

Second, support the long-term survival in the region of these ancient indigenous religious and ethnic communities. In Iraq, the Christian population has declined by more than 80 percent, and in Syria, it has declined by almost 70 percent. American policy should recognize the important differences in the situations of those fleeing violence and those targeted for genocide, and quite frankly, we should prioritize the latter. Consider this analogy: After World War II, there were approximately 50 million refugees, but only a small fraction were Jews. Yet the world understood that Jews who had survived genocide faced a qualitatively different situation and deserved heightened consideration. The same is true today for the indigenous minorities of the region. They have an indisputable right to live in their country in whatever region of it they wish. Depending on the circumstances, this may mean that they will live where they are originally from or where they find themselves now, but as survivors of an ongoing genocide, they deserve to be prioritized in American policymaking decisions.

Third, punish the perpetrators of genocide and crimes against humanity. The United States should support action by the U.N. Security Council to refer key perpetrators of genocide for prosecution. Equally important, we should support the Iraqi Government and the Kurdish Regional Government's adjudication of the cases of thousands of ISIS fighters and supporters who remain in local detention centers. This will assist in the important work of obtaining and preserving evidence of genocide.

Fourth, we should assist victims of genocide in attaining refugee status. The news report as of last week indicated that of the 499

Syrian refugees admitted to the U.S. in May, not one was explicitly listed as being Christian or as coming from any of the groups targeted for genocide. We must ask, how long will this situation be allowed to continue? The U.S. should appropriate funding and work with the U.N. High Commissioner for Refugees to make provisions for locating and providing status to individuals, such as Yazidis and Christians, that have been targeted for genocide. As I mentioned earlier, many of these genocide survivors fear going into official U.N. refugee camps where they are targeted. Thus, they are overlooked and find it nearly impossible to acquire official refugee status or to immigrate.

Congress should act now. Senator Tom Cotton has introduced the Religious Persecution Relief Act, S. 2708, to provide for overlooked minorities in the prioritization of refugees. We support this bill, and we urge its passage.

Fifth, prepare now for the foreseeable human rights challenges as ISIS--controlled territory is liberated by ensuring that Christians and other minorities have equal rights to decide their future, and obviously, this is going to happen very soon as a result of what is happening in Fallujah and Mosul. We should prepare now for the consequences of the liberation of ISIS-controlled areas. We are likely to see another humanitarian crisis as thousands of civilians flee the fighting or return to their former communities when the fighting ceases.

There has been much debate concerning plans for victims of genocide in Iraq. Some have argued for returning people safely to the Nineveh region; others that they should be allowed to stay in Kurdistan; still others that they should be allowed to immigrate. But these are not necessarily ultimately exclusive competing proposals. People should be allowed to decide their own future, and when they do, we should work to ensure that they are treated with fairness, dignity and equality. This also means that it will be increasingly important to ensure that the property rights and claims of minority groups are respected.

And, finally, sixth, promote the establishment of internationally agreed-upon standards of human rights and religious freedom as conditions for our humanitarian and military assistance. The United States should advocate for full and equal rights for religious and ethnic minorities in the region in exchange for our military and humanitarian aid. A necessary first step to prevent genocide is to overcome the social and legal inequality that is its breeding ground. We should not accept one standard for human rights in the region and another standard for the rest of the world. The rich tapestry of religious pluralism in the region must be preserved now, or it will be lost forever. With its loss will come increasing instability and threats to our own national security and that of the world.

We have a unique opportunity, and some would say a unique responsibility, to protect the victims of genocide. The United States can provide such protection with a policy that includes the principles outlined above.

Mr. Chairman, we thank you very much for your leadership and that of the other members of the committee.

[The prepared statement of Mr. Anderson follows:]

Opening Statement of

Mr. Carl A. Anderson

Supreme Knight

Knights of Columbus

Before the Subcommittee on Africa, Global Health

Global Human Rights and International Organizations

of the

Committee on Foreign Affairs

U.S. House of Representatives

At a hearing titled

The ISIS Genocide Declaration: What Next?

May 26, 2016

Thank you for the opportunity to appear before this subcommittee and to discuss the next steps that need to be taken needed to protect the survivors of ongoing genocide in Iraq and Syria. Let me begin by saying that the House of Representatives, the State Department and the United States Commission on International Religious Freedom are all to be commended for the important step of declaring the situation confronting Christians and other religious minorities in the Middle East genocide.

The world's greatest humanitarian crisis since World War II is unfolding now in the Middle East. In addition to millions of refugees, many of the region's indigenous communities now face extinction. These communities may disappear in less than a decade. But their fate is not inevitable. The United States can avert this unfolding tragedy.

A unique historical moment

Around the world, people of good will, Muslim and non-Muslim alike, wish to differentiate themselves from the horrific and violent theology espoused by ISIS.

It is certainly true that such extremists make up a small percentage of Muslims overall. But among the world's billion Muslims, the majority simply want to raise their families in peace and are scandalized by what ISIS is doing in the name of Islam.

Prominent Islamic leaders and scholars from around the world have recently taken an important step in the Marrakesh Declaration.[1] Attempts such as this, which seek to align Islam with the Universal Declaration of Human Rights should be supported.

At the same time, it is clear that Christians, and other indigenous minorities, are experiencing genocide, at the hands of the Islamic State and related groups. Their plight is now at the top of the world's agenda in a way that it never has been before.

These factors together create an unparalleled opportunity for the United States, and for all those opposed to ISIS' radical vision – Muslims and non-Muslims alike – to advance an agenda of equality, justice, peace, and accountability in the region.

Six principles for sound policy in the region

The United States can avert the extinction of indigenous religious and ethnic communities in Iraq and Syria with a policy that contains the following six principles:

(1)   Increase aid and ensure that it actually reaches those most in need;

We are reliably informed that official government and U.N. aid does not reach the Christian genocide survivors in Iraq and Syria.

Repeatedly, we hear from Church leaders in the region that Christians – and other genocide survivors – are last in line for assistance from governments. Significantly, the Archdiocese of Erbil, where most Iraqi Christians now live, receives no money from any government whatsoever. If assistance from outside Church affiliated agencies ends in Erbil, Christians there will face a catastrophic humanitarian tragedy within 30 days. The situation is similar in Syria, according to Christian leaders there.

---

[1] http://www.marrakeshdeclaration.org/

Those who face genocide are a tiny fraction of the population. They often must avoid official refugee camps because they are targeted for violence there by extremists. As a result, these minorities often do not get "official" aid. This will continue to be the reality unless specific action is taken to bring the aid to where these minorities are forced to reside by continuing violence.

The Knights of Columbus and others private sources have responded to this situation. Since 2014, we have raised more than $10.5 million for relief, assisting Christians and other internally displaced persons and refugees in Iraq, Syria, Jordan, and Lebanon. We have partnered with dioceses and religious agencies working in the region to provide general relief, food, clothing, shelter, education, and medical care. In doing so we assist both Christians and non-Christians. We are also working with church entities to ensure that they are making use of all government or U.N. resources available.

But non-governmental organizations can only do so much. Government aid is essential to the long-term survival of these indigenous religious and ethnic minorities. It is urgent that Congress appropriate funding to save those who have escaped genocide. I urge you to consider special emergency appropriations, however modest, to improve the humanitarian conditions on the ground in Iraq.[2]

This funding, whatever the vehicle, should come with mechanisms in place —reporting requirements and oversight—to ensure that American aid does not get diverted from its intended purpose.

(2)   Support the long-term survival in the region of these ancient indigenous religious and ethnic communities;

In Iraq, the Christians population has declined by more than 80 percent, and in Syria by nearly 70 percent.

American policy should recognize the important differences in the situations of those fleeing violence and those targeted for genocide. And we should prioritize the latter.

Consider this analogy. After World War II, there were approximately 50 million refugees, and only a small fraction were Jews. Yet the world understood that Jews, who had survived genocide, faced a qualitatively different situation, and deserved heightened consideration.

The same is true today for the indigenous religious and ethnic minorities of the region. They have an indisputable right to live in their country – in whatever region of it they wish. Depending on the circumstances, this may mean where they are originally from, or where they find themselves now, but as survivors of an ongoing genocide, they deserve to be prioritized, not left behind by American policy decisions.

(3)   Punish the perpetrators of genocide and crimes against humanity;

The United States should support action by the U.N. Security Council to refer key perpetrators of genocide for prosecution. Equally important, we should support the Iraqi Central

---

[2] U.S. State Department and U.N. personnel have mentioned the State Department Economic Support Fund and the United Nations Funding Facility for Immediate Stabilization as two relevant, among others.

Government and the Kurdish Regional Government's adjudication of the cases of thousands of ISIS fighters and supporters who currently remain in local detention centers.

As the population of captured ISIS fighters increases, local detention centers and jails risk becoming their own humanitarian issue.[3] The need to improve this situation cannot be overstated.

Additionally, although substantial evidence of genocide exists, the United States should cooperate in taking further action to develop additional documentation and preservation before physical evidence is lost. Appropriations intended to assist in the adjudication of ISIS fighters will be critical in the coming months.[4]

(4)   Assist victims of genocide in attaining refugee status.

A news report last week indicated that of the 499 Syrian refugees admitted to the U.S. in May, not one was listed as being Christian or as explicitly coming from any of the groups targeted for genocide.[5] How long will this situation be allowed to continue?

The U.S. should appropriate funding and work with the U.N. High Commissioner for Refugees to make provisions for locating and providing status to individuals – such as Yezidis and Christians – that have been targeted for genocide. Many of these genocide survivors fear going into official U.N. refugee camps, where they are targeted. Thus they are overlooked, and find it nearly impossible to acquire official refugee status or immigrate.[6]

Congress should act now. Senator Tom Cotton has introduced the Religious Persecution Relief Act, S. 2708, to provide for overlooked minorities in the prioritization of refugees. We support this bill and urge its passage.

(5)   Prepare now for foreseeable human rights challenges as ISIS-controlled territory is liberated by ensuring that Christians and other minorities have equal rights to decide their future;

We should prepare now for the consequences of the liberation of ISIS controlled areas, including Mosul and the Nineveh Region, as well as regions in Syria. We are likely to see another humanitarian crisis as civilians flee the fighting or return to their former communities when fighting ceases.

---

[3] *See*, Charlie Savage, et. al. *Lack of Plan for ISIS Detainees Raises Human Rights Concerns*, NEW YORK TIMES, (May 11, 2016), at
http://www.nytimes.com/2016/05/12/world/middleeast/lack-of-plan-for-isis-detainees-raises-human-rights-concerns.html?_r=0.

[4] Congress can look to fund the State Department Office of Global Criminal Justice and the Human Rights Defenders Fund to help meet this need.

[5] *See*, Patrick Goodenough, *Record 499 Syrian Refugees Admitted to US So Far in May Includes No Christians*, CNSNEWS.COM, May 23, 2016, at http://www.cnsnews.com/news/article/patrick-goodenough/may-brings-biggest-monthly-number-syrian-refugee-arrivals-conflict.

[6] *Fulfilling the Humanitarian Imperative: Assisting Victims of ISIS Violence: Hearing Before the Subcomm. on Africa, Global Health, Global H. Rights and Intl. Orgs. of the H. Foreign Aff. Comm.*, 114th Cong. (2015) (Statement of Carl A. Anderson, Supreme Knight of the Knights of Columbus).
http://docs.house.gov/meetings/FA/FA16/20151209/104273/HHRG-114-FA16-Wstate-AndersonC-20151209.pdf.

There has been much debate concerning plans for victims of genocide in Iraq. Some have argued for returning people safely to the Nineveh Region, others that they should be allowed to stay in Kurdistan, still others that they be allowed to immigrate. But these are not necessarily mutually exclusive, competing proposals. People should be allowed to decide their own future. And when they do, we should work to ensure they are treated with fairness, dignity and equality. This also means that it will be increasingly important to ensure that the property rights and claims of minority groups are respected.

(6)   Promote the establishment of internationally agreed upon standards of human rights and religious freedom as conditions for humanitarian and military assistance.

The United States should advocate for full and equal rights for religious and ethnic minorities in the region in exchange for our military and humanitarian aid. A necessary first step to prevent genocide is to overcome the social and legal inequality that is its breeding ground.

Religious hatred, discrimination and second-class citizenship too often constitute a way of life in the region—and it is a way of life that is an antecedent to genocide. We cannot accept one standard for human rights in the region and another standard for the rest of the world.

The guarantees in the Universal Declaration of Human Rights – and the First and Fourteenth amendments to our own constitution – regarding equality under the law and freedom of speech and religion must become a reality for all citizens of Iraq, Syria and elsewhere throughout the region.

Conclusion

The rich tapestry of religious pluralism in the region must be preserved now or it will be lost forever. With its loss will come increased instability and threats to our own security and that of the world.

We have a unique opportunity—and some would say, unique responsibility--to protect the victims of genocide. The United States can provide such protection with a policy that includes the principles outlined above. Mr. Chairman, thank you very much for your leadership and that of the members of this subcommittee.

Mr. SMITH. Mr. Anderson, thank you so very much for your comments, the very tangible support you are providing to the at-risk minorities, especially Christians. And those six points, they are very, very, very well thought out.

I would like to now recognize Mr. Hamasaeed, and thank you for being here and for your testimony.

STATEMENT OF MR. SARHANG HAMASAEED, SENIOR PROGRAM OFFICER, MIDDLE EAST AND AFRICA PROGRAMS, U.S. INSTITUTE OF PEACE

Mr. HAMASAEED. Chairman Smith, Ranking Member Bass, and members of the subcommittee, thank you for the opportunity to testify before you today. I am testifying as a senior program officer of the U.S. Institute of Peace. The views expressed here are my own and do not represent that of the institute. USIP works extensively and closely with Iraqi minorities, specifically religious minorities. We support them by establishing an organization called the Alliance for Iraqi Minorities so that they have the capability to represent themselves, and so, in that vein, a lot of what I mention today is coming from experience directly engaging and trying to help those minorities.

Definitely, the minorities in Iraq need all the support that they can get as well as other communities, nonminority communities, in Iraq.

The dilemma of the religious minorities is not something new. I think it is important to look into some of the history so that we can inform solutions that will, to see if they will work and how do we prepare for those. The reality is that the minorities have, over the past few decades, been caught in between the conflicts and the problems of actors that they were not a part of. They didn't choose those conflicts, but they were affected by those conflicts. And ISIS is not a product, and what they have done is not a product of today. ISIS is a cause of atrocity, but it also is a symptom of failure of governance and the space it has created resulting from the political divisions among the big actors in Iraq and the region.

So it is true that the minorities have suffered probably the most at the hands of ISIS in the sense that they came under attack, for displacement, for genocide, and also chemical attacks against the Turkomans in the Taza district of Kirkuk. The Yazidis have had their women and others taken as sex slaves. The Christians have been labeled, their houses labeled, and they came under specific attack.

Then the question comes: What was the response? The specific question that was addressed to me to talk about was the response of the Government of Iraq and the Kurdistan Regional Government. And to look at this, you can look at this from the perspective of a glass half full or a glass half empty. The reality is that the minorities believe that the Government of Iraq and the Kurdistan Regional Government have not been able to protect them; that they have been displaced, and they have been affected. But it is also true that the Kurdistan Regional Government and the Government of Iraq have provided camps and shelters and provided food and assistance. They were also supported by the Iraqi community—which

I think is important—and they have to recognize their efforts in absorbing this crisis and the problems here.

But the reality is that the scope of the problem is well beyond the capacity of one single actor, one single government, or one single community. It requires a collective action. And there is a sense of fatigue for the years of displacement, especially since 2003. The limited capacity of the government and other actors needs to be taken into consideration into what assistance is provided.

I think that there is a need for rethinking the assistance that is given to the minorities and their situation. On protection, the call for protection is not something new. This has been, as you mentioned, Mr. Chairman, there has been a call by the minorities to address this for a long time. And the kind of risk that the minorities are confronted with, they are existential threats that threaten their collective well-being. It is also a direct risk to their security as individuals and communities.

So the risk of revenge, I would like to single out. We talked about the post-return. There is a scenario of protracted displacement, which will be a scenario that we have to deal with. In the 2006, 2007 peak of violence in Iraq, about 1 million people never returned home. And the current 3.3 million people that are displaced, about 1 million of them minorities, they will likely not be able to return for quite some time because of problems that are on the ground, and the revenge is killing and the potential violence coming in those areas is a potential risk to them.

The U.S. Institute of Peace has worked on models that help the return of IDPs and prevent violence. We have done this in the context of Salahuddin and the Speicher massacre that ISIS perpetrated against the Shia cadets and soldiers who were in that camp. We facilitated dialogue among the tribes, and we have been able to mitigate the violence and prevent killing and facilitate the return of IDPs. Tikrit right now has about 150,000 people who have returned since May of last year.

The same kind of effort will be needed in the context of the minorities because there are several layers of conflict that need to be addressed: Risks coming from existential threats like ISIL; then there are risks that will come from competition over scarce resources; and there will be risks coming from just tensions of some of the minorities considering what has happened to them by some of their Arab neighbors. There are minority-minority tensions that need to be addressed. There are Arab minority issues and Kurdish-Kurdish issues that need to be addressed. There is a need for conflict resolution to help them with the long-term viability.

The minorities have the organizations and the capabilities to help themselves. They have been a partner and a voice for the minorities over the years. The Alliance of Iraqi Minorities has worked with the national government and with the Kurdistan Regional Government to pass legislation and make sure their issues have been prioritized. And they could continue to play that role. But at the end of the day, the scope of the need, the magnitude of the problem, will require more than what has been provided to date. I cannot emphasize enough the need for international support for early detection and action on those warning signs that the minorities have been giving us.

It goes without saying that actually solving the bigger problems of Iraq will go a long way in helping the minorities over the long-term to stay safe and not to be attacked. While the minorities will be able to develop the capabilities to provide local security, larger existential threats coming from problems like ISIL, will require the help and the support of the Iraqi Government and the Kurdistan Regional Government and the larger communities around the minorities. So it is important to put emphasis on, how do you rebuild those relationships? How do we put mechanisms in place that will prevent those kinds of attacks?

I think the capacity is limited and the peaceful coexistence is the emphasis that we need to put in as a mechanism. Civil society organizations have been a good vehicle to help the Government of Iraq and the international community. They will need help in both a scenario of return, but also a scenario of protracted displacement, to prevent host community tensions as well.

So, with that, I will stop.

And thank you, Mr. Chairman, and members of the subcommittee. I look forward to your questions.

[The prepared statement of Mr. Hamasaeed follows:]

United States Institute of Peace

The ISIS Genocide Declaration: What Next?

Testimony before the

House Foreign Affairs Subcommittee on Africa, Global Health,

Global Human Rights, and International Organizations

Sarhang Hamasaeed

Senior Program Officer

United States Institute of Peace

May 26, 2016

Introduction

Chairman Smith, Ranking Member Bass, members of the Subcommittee, thank you for the opportunity to testify before you today on the current situation of religious minorities in Iraq, efforts of the Government of Iraq (GoI) and the Kurdistan Regional Government to provide assistance, and steps that can be taken to help improve the situation of minorities in Iraq.

I testify before you today as a Senior Program Officer of the United States Institute of Peace (USIP). The views expressed here represent my own and not those of USIP. USIP was established by Congress over 30 years ago as an independent, national institute dedicated to the proposition that peace is possible, practical, and essential to our national and global security. The Institute engages directly in conflict zones and provides tools, analysis, training, education, and resources to those working for peace. USIP has worked extensively with minority groups in Iraq, including supporting the establishment of the Alliance of Iraqi Minorities in 2011 to strengthen their joint efforts to advocate for their rights as citizens.

I commend Congress' continued interest in this issue, especially in light of Secretary of State John Kerry's March 17 designation of the atrocities against minority religious groups in Iraq, including Shia Muslims, as genocide. Members of the U.S. Congress, as you know, have sponsored legislation calling for the same and appealing for the U.S. Government and the international community to take more action to protect religious minorities in Iraq. The ethnic and religious minorities, as well as non-minorities of Iraq need all the help they can get.

The American democracy is proof that ethnically and religiously diverse society can work. The Middle East is one of the most ethnically and religiously diverse societies on the planet. Iraq, home to ancient civilizations, has had a particularly rich mosaic of peoples. Although it is easy to grow despondent about the ethnic and religious cleansing that has taken place, it is still possible to envision an Iraq and a Middle East with a mosaic society at peace. But it takes commitment and methodical work, resources and time to provide alternatives to violence.

My testimony will address:

- How religious minorities are affected by the larger conflicts within Iraq, in the region, and among international powers. Unless those conflicts are resolved or at least mitigated, the minorities caught in the maelstrom will continue to be vulnerable.
- A reminder of attacks on Iraqi minorities that decimated their numbers even before the rampage of the self-styled Islamic State (also known as ISIS, ISIL, Daesh, or other names), and the collective toll over the decades.
- The record of Iraq's minorities in working to improve their own economic, social and political conditions in the country, and in responding in the aftermath of the ISIS attacks. The repeated mobilization of these communities to help themselves illustrates the potential when they receive the international community's support.
- The response of the Iraqi and Kurdistan Regional governments, the United States, and the international community to help religious minorities—and what supporters can do moving forward.

The Dilemma of Religious Minorities: Ensnared in Larger Conflicts

Religious minorities in Iraq have been adversely affected by conflicts repeatedly over the decades, from Saddam Hussein's destruction of thousands of villages in the 1980s to direct attacks from ISIS's predecessors, al-Qaeda in Iraq (AQI, aka al-Qaeda in Mesopotamia), which morphed into the Islamic State of Iraq (ISI) in 2006 and ISIS in 2013.

According to the International Organization for Migration (IOM), the conflict involving ISIS has displaced more than 3.3 million people in Iraq, including some 1 million minorities. ISIS continues to control or threaten minority areas in Iraq's Nineveh Province.

As a result, the number of religious minorities in Iraq has dropped precipitously. While there has been no census in Iraq for decades, Christian groups in Iraq estimate their numbers have declined from about 1.5 million in 2003 to less than one-third of that now. The Yazidis cite more than 70 acts of genocide perpetrated against them throughout their history. These onslaughts have left only about 1 million Yazidis worldwide, including between 500,000 and 700,000 in Iraq. The Sabean-Mandaeans have been less directly targeted by ISIS, perhaps only because they live further away, but their numbers too have fallen to a few thousand worldwide, most within Iraq. No Jews are known to be left in areas controlled by the Iraqi government or by ISIS, and only a small number of Jews—probably in the hundreds or fewer—remain in the Kurdistan Region of Iraq.

Religious minorities in Iraq have long faced existential threats largely because of broader conflicts, circumstances, and actors outside their control and because of genocidal ideologies or tactics that predate ISIS.

Sunni-Shia and Arab-Persian competition produced an eight-year war between Iraq and Iran from 1980 to 1988 that cost the lives of more than 600,000 people[1] with many minorities caught in the middle. Also in the 1980s, Saddam Hussein and the Baath Party perpetrated genocide against the Kurds; used chemical weapons, rape and torture against innocent civilians; and destroyed over 4,500 villages. ISIS continues to perpetrate similar acts today. ISIS has taken thousands of Yazidi and Christian women and young girls as sex-slaves from Sinjar and other areas of Nineveh, used chemical weapons that killed minority Turkumen in Taza district, and massacred as many as 1,700 mostly Shia military cadets and soldiers near Tikrit.

ISIS is both a cause of atrocities and a symptom of governance failure resulting from political division and competition for power among Iraq's main ethno-sectarian forces (mainly the Shia, Sunnis, and the Kurds) and their regional backers. The group also grew from the belief that the use of force and violence are the only means to win or to resolve differences.

In Iraq, religious minorities have been caught in disputes between the Government of Iraq and the Kurdistan Regional Government over internal boundaries and the political agendas of big political parties. Of course religious minorities also have had their own internal disputes, such as

---

[1] PRIO Battle Deaths Dataset - Lacina, Bethany & Nils Petter Gleditsch. 2005. 'Monitoring Trends in Global Combat: A New Dataset of Battle Deaths', European Journal of Population 21(2–3): 145–166.

one that came close to triggering violence in 2012 between the Christians and the Shabak in the town of Bartella in the Nineveh Plain, a sweeping, multi-ethnic area in the Nineveh Province.

Iraqi and Kurdistan Regional Governments Response to the Needs of Displaced Minorities

Security

Failures of the political process and exclusionary policies of political leaders, such as former Prime Minister Nouri al-Maliki, triggered the current cycle of conflict in Iraq. Internally displaced people (IDP's), especially religious minorities, see the government of Iraq and the Iraqi Security Forces (ISF) as having failed to protect them, especially after official Iraqi military units abandoned their locations and weapons in Nineveh and other places in the summer of 2014, allowing ISIS to overrun large swaths of northwestern Iraq in a matter of a few days. Religious minorities, particularly the Yazidis and Christians, also feel the Kurdistan Regional Government failed to protect them in Sinjar and other areas of the Nineveh Plain during that devastating period.

Yet the vast majority of Iraqi minorities are now taking refuge in areas protected by the Kurdish Peshmerga that control not only the autonomous region, but also much of the Nineveh Plain and Kirkuk Province. Other armed groups, like the Syrian Kurdish Democratic Union Party, also play a role protecting minorities in some liberated areas of Nineveh. But it is the Peshmerga, supported by the U.S.-led Global Coalition to Counter ISIS that is the primary force preventing and rolling back ISIS advances in minority areas.

A smaller number of minorities live in areas under the control of the Iraqi government, where security is provided by the Iraqi Security Forces, Iraqi police, and the Popular Mobilization Forces (PMF, also known as al-Hashd al-Shaaby or Shia militias). Fundamentally, however, minorities trust neither the Government of Iraq nor the Kurdistan Regional Government to protect them in liberated areas. Still, minorities and other displaced Iraqis currently living in the Kurdistan Region or parts of Iraq outside the control of ISIS, like Baghdad or the country's south, are at least safer.

Displacement: Magnitude, Capacity to Handle, and Fatigue

In addition to providing security, the Iraqi and Kurdistan Regional governments have aided IDPs by setting up camps for shelter, offering limited financial support, and supplying food and health care. The U.N., international aid organizations and foreign governments support those efforts, as well as operating their own direct programs. Still, these efforts continue to fall woefully short of the needs for shelter, food, health care, education, and psycho-social support to deal with trauma.

The government of Iraq provided cash to IDPs in a one-time payment of 1 million Iraqi Dinars—about $833. But corruption, lack of required documentation, frequent movement of some of the IDPs, and the limited capacity of the Iraqi Ministry of Migration and Displacement Affairs has resulted in cash payments or even monthly food rations from the Public Distribution System of Iraq being delayed or not delivered at all.

The Kurdistan Region shelters about 1.5 million displaced Iraqis, including minorities and others, as well as some 250,000 Syrian refugees. The region has hosted IDPs for most of the period since the 2003 U.S. invasion, especially from 2006 to 2008, when religious or sectarian violence reached record levels in Iraq.

It is estimated that 1 million IDPs from the 2006-2008 period never returned home, a good portion of them staying in the Kurdistan Region. In 2013, displacement accelerated again and peaked in 2014,[2] as many Arabs and religious minorities from Anbar, Salahaddin, and Nineveh fled to Iraqi Kurdistan. This time the numbers were unprecedented, putting enormous strain on the Kurdistan region and its governing structures. Many places of worship, schools, public buildings, and unfinished buildings became shelters for IDPs. Significant support came from local citizens who hosted families, donated food and clothes, and even provided homes rent-free. Civil society organizations in the Kurdistan Region and the rest of Iraq, including the minority communities inside and outside Iraq, have been pivotal in their support for the IDPs, including with food, clothes, health care, education and psycho-social support.

Given the protracted displacement, the economic hardships triggered by the drop in oil prices, and internal political gridlock, the IDPs and their host communities have exhausted their resources.

The authorities, people, organizations, and private companies that have stepped up again and again in this crisis will not be able to help IDPs much more, increasing the risks of escalating tensions and competition over dwindling resources. The international relief system is severely strained and struggles to raise the necessary levels of funding to cope with the proliferation of humanitarian crises in Iraq, Syria, and elsewhere in the world.

The U.S. and Global Responses

The Department of Defense has already provided $3.1 billion in assistance to the Iraqi government in support of activities to counter ISIS. The U.S. currently supplies air power, command and control, and other security support, training, sustainment, and logistics. Secretary Carter recently announced that the Department of Defense will provide a $415 million package of financial assistance to the Peshmerga in response to a request from the fiscally strapped Kurdistan Regional Government. In anticipation of the operation to retake Mosul, the Pentagon also announced increases in the number of American military advisors and additional equipment made available to Iraqi forces.[3] The United States has also contributed more than $750m in humanitarian assistance to the Iraqi people since the ISIS conflict began in 2014.[4]

---

[2] IOM Displacement Tracking Matrix, DTM Round 44, May 2016 Accessed at: http://iomiraq.net/dtm-page
[3] Carter: Next Steps in Iraq ISIL Fight Include More Troops, Military Equipment, Accessed at:
http://www.defense.gov/News-Article-View/Article/737764/carter-next-steps-in-iraq-ISIS-fight-include-more-troops-military-equipment
[4] US Department of State – New Humanitarian Assistance for Iraq, Accessed at:
http://www.state.gov/r/pa/prs/ps/2016/04/255613.htm

In addition, in June 2015, the international community pledged $100 million to fund stabilization efforts following the establishment of the U.N. Development Program's Funding Facility for Immediate Stabilization (FFIS), the global mechanism created to quickly respond to targeted stabilization needs in liberated areas through service delivery, community reconciliation, capacity building, and infrastructure development. As of March 31, the FFIS had received $67 million. Of that, $46 million has been spent or obligated for expenditure. [5]

Rethinking Assistance to Religious Minorities

Protection

The religious minorities, and even some ethnic minorities, call for international protection in some form. Calls by many religious minorities for safe zones and autonomous zones are not new, and occurred repeatedly even before the emergence of ISIS in response to other attacks outlined earlier. The call for autonomous zones also is inspired, at least in part, by provisions for decentralization and self-administered units enshrined in the Iraqi constitution. It is, therefore, important to determine in each case what problems might be addressed by safe and/or autonomous zones, and, conversely, what problems such areas might create or aggravate.

It risks stating the obvious to point out that a genuine lessening of the Middle East's underlying conflicts would go a long way toward improving security for the region's minorities in the long term. In the meantime, minorities need physical security to protect them against existential threats like ISIS, and cultural security to preserve their communities, religions, languages and culture. Enabling minorities to police and protect their own areas, and take part in Iraqi and Kurdistan Regional Government security institutions would help, but they will always need the support of those governments.

The recent violent conflicts in Iraq have militarized society to an alarming extent. Weapons have flooded into communities, and many citizens see no option but violence to resolve conflicts. Christians, Yazidis and Shabak have taken up arms, and formed their own military units under the command of the Kurdish Peshmerga, the Iraqi Security Forces, the Popular Mobilization Forces, other Kurdish troops such as the Syrian Kurdish Democratic Union Party. In some cases, religious minority groups have formed their own armed groups independently. While it may be tempting to consider these actions as a mere effort at self-defense, they carry the greater risk of pulling minorities more directly into existing and future armed conflicts, as well as complicating future attempts to disarm and reestablish government control. And yet other actors in Iraqi and regional conflicts will always have greater numbers and more powerful weapons. The dilemma of minorities could be further aggravated.

Return of IDPs to Liberated Areas

---

[5] UNDP Iraq Funding Facility for Immediate Stabilization Quarterly Progress Report Q1 – Year 2016. Accessed at: http://www.iq.undp.org/content/iraq/en/home/library/Stabilization/funding-facility-for-immediate-stabilization--ffis--progress-rep.html

Minority areas in the Nineveh Plain and Nineveh Province overall remain under ISIS control or threat of attack, and the pace of recapturing these locations remains slow. Liberating and securing Mosul City is months away, probably more. Even when areas are freed from ISIS rule, the return of IDPs will be delayed while mines are cleared, basic services such as electricity and water are restored and trust of security forces is rebuilt. Without that achievement and accompanying guarantees of protection, the minorities likely will continue to emigrate to the West. Even after their communities are recaptured by friendly forces, a good number may still sell whatever land and properties they have and leave the country in search of a more sustainable peace.

UNDP estimated in late 2015 that 275,000 Yazidis from Sinjar and Sinuni towns are still displaced.[6] In Sinuni, which was recaptured from ISIS in 2014, only 20 percent of the population has returned, a process delayed by demining as well as the persistent security threats from the proximity to the current front line. The majority of Yazidis depend on farming and herding for their livelihoods, yet agricultural equipment was destroyed or stolen and farm land remains contaminated by mines. Basic public services like electricity and water are still lacking. And the return could be complicated by still more displacement. The Kurdistan Regional Government expects to receive between 300,000 and 500,000 displaced people when Mosul is recaptured.[7]

Another risk is that of revenge violence when ISIS is driven from areas it has controlled and displaced residents return with suspicions that those who stayed were complicit with the extremists. Nineveh Province will require multi-layered conflict mitigation and reconciliation to prevent renewed cycles of violence based on retribution, and to restore and sustain social cohesion. Such work likely would need to cover disputes among the minorities themselves, and between the minorities and Arab tribes, Kurds and Arabs, minorities and Kurds, potentially among Kurds, and the communities and the state.

USIP has successfully implemented interventions in both Iraq and Syria that address these kinds of community reconciliation issues.

- USIP brokered a reconciliation pact in the then-volatile district of Mahmoudiyah, south of Baghdad, between Sunni and Shia tribes in 2007.
- USIP and the Network of Iraqi Facilitators that USIP helped establish provided trained dialogue facilitators to ease tensions and prevent violence between Shabak and Christian communities in Bartella in Nineveh Province in 2012.
- USIP and the facilitators network, as well as another Iraqi partner, Sanad for Peacebuilding, forestalled revenge acts of violence in 2015 after the recapture of Tikrit, preventing a renewed cycle of violence over the 2014 massacre of 1,700 military cadets and soldiers, most of them Shia, at the nearby Camp Speicher military base. USIP's

---

[6] UNDP Iraq Funding Facility for Immediate Stabilization Quarterly Progress Report Q4 – Year 2015. Accessed at: http://www.iq.undp.org/content/dam/iraq/docs/Stabilization/UNDP%20IQ-
%20Stabilization%20FFIS%20Progress%20Report%20Q4%202015-%20201601.pdf?download
[7] Al-Jazeera Iraq's humanitarian workers brace for Mosul influx. Accessed at:
http://www.aljazeera.com/news/2016/04/iraq-humanitarian-workers-brace-mosul-influx-160410105114219.html

stabilization model, which involves third-party mediation and the engagement of key national and local leaders, produced an agreement in which tribal leaders committed to disavow members of their tribes who had been involved in the massacre. This agreement culminated in the initial return of 400 displaced Sunni families to Tikrit in June 2015. IOM reports that 158,412 IDPs have returned since then.

USIP is supporting a similar process in Yathrib in Salahaddin Province, and is working with the National Reconciliation Committee of the Iraqi Prime Minister's Office to support such efforts in Anbar and Nineveh provinces. USIP also has trained security and civilian personnel of the Kurdistan Regional Government and civil society organizations to address IDP issues with sensitivity to the causes and effects of conflict, with the aim of preventing violence among IDPs and between IDPs and their host communities.

Resilience of the Minorities

Despite the atrocities that are all too apparent and that must be stopped, it is crucial to remember that the religious minorities of Iraq have remarkable strengths and capabilities. As mentioned earlier, USIP helped establish, and continues to support, the Alliance of Iraqi Minorities (AIM), a coalition of civil society organizations that provides a voice for minority groups. AIM was formed in 2011 and is comprised of 13 non-governmental organizations representing the country's Christians, Faily Kurds, Kakayee, Sabean-Mandaeans, Shabaks, and Yazidis. AIM has a board of directors, a general assembly and an advisory body that includes a Baha'i member as well as other minorities.

Among AIM's many accomplishments, in 2014, before the ISIS onslaught, AIM partnered with the United Nations to organize a national conference on all Iraqi minorities. That culminated in the adoption of a national declaration and action plan to inform the advocacy of the minorities, and the work of the Iraqi Government and the international community to protect the minorities. Their most notable accomplishment occurred just last year, when AIM contributed to the Kurdistan Regional Government's law on minorities, as well as the region's draft constitution, to ensure minorities were properly represented and protected. AIM members played an instrumental role in helping the minority IDPs, as they were being displaced, through providing shelter, food, and informing the international community of the developments. Earlier, in 2012 and 2013, AIM won changes in Iraq's national budget law to allow for more equitable allocations to their geographic regions, and helped draft curriculum changes in Iraqi textbooks to mention minorities and include text from their holy books and literature for the first time.

AIM continues to serve as a strong voice for minorities in Iraq and remains a critical source of information for international supporters, specifically the U.S. Government through USIP, the U.S. Embassy in Baghdad, the U.N., Iraqi authorities, and the Kurdistan Regional Government.

Recommendations

I recommend the following to address the current situation of religious minorities in Iraq:

- The most certain way to protect and preserve the future of religious minorities in Iraq is to resolve the larger conflicts of Iraq and their international supporters. At their core, a resolution of these conflicts will require political processes and solutions, supplemented by security and economic measures. Such efforts require an active and leading role from the United States to facilitate peace processes and provide technical and resource assistance to implement agreements.

- The Government of Iraq, the Kurdistan Regional Government, the United States, the United Nations, and other international actors must adopt early detection mechanisms— and the resulting necessary actions—to prevent atrocities against both majority and minority communities. Religious minorities in Iraq have been warning about threats to their communities for many years, and security indicators gave ample warning about the risk that Iraqi security forces would collapse, and that Mosul would fall.

- Iraqi minorities trust neither the Government of Iraq nor the Kurdistan Regional Government to protect them in areas recaptured from ISIS. The attacks at Sinjar and other areas of the Nineveh Plain, particularly against Yazidis and Christians, and the unprecedented social, political and financial strain of the resulting displacement and global economic crises, have left a legacy that will require intense efforts to address. Mechanisms are necessary to ease tensions and repair ties among the minorities themselves, among Kurds, and between the minorities and Arab tribes, Kurds and Arabs, minorities and Kurds, and the communities and the state. A good place to start would be the local conflicts in the Nineveh Province and Nineveh Plain. Providing civilian mechanisms for all the parties to identify needs, prioritize them, and engage each other and the international community for ways to implement the agreed solutions would resolve many core problems and serve as an example to Iraqi minorities and non-minorities in other areas.

- The Iraqis lack the needed technical and financial capacity, especially given the significant public budget deficit due to the drop in oil prices, to manage the multiple challenges facing them, including political wrangling, public outrage towards the government, the military campaign against ISIS, and humanitarian and economic crises. The Kurdistan Regional Government, the Government of Iraq, and the minority communities need help to rebuild schools, hospitals, roads, and other key infrastructure in areas recaptured from ISIS. This could include helping the minorities help themselves the same way the Alliance of Iraqi Minorities is doing —to influence legislation, tap into national and local budgets, and attract international support to help them address their needs.

- Given the likelihood that the current record displacements of people will be protracted, the United States and the international community should support programs in conflict prevention and peaceful co-existence for liberated areas, as well as in the communities of the Kurdistan Region and the rest of Iraq that have so generously sheltered those displaced.

Thank you, again, for the Subcommittee's continued focus and attention to this critical issue. I look forward to answering your questions.

The views expressed in this testimony are those of the author and not the U.S. Institute of Peace.

Mr. SMITH. Mr. Hamasaeed, I am going to say thank you very much for your testimony, which was very extensive. I have read it, and other members, I am sure, have read it.

Without objection, your and all of the distinguished witnesses' full statements and any information you would like to attach to it will be made a part of the record. So thank you for that testimony.

Mr. Oram.

STATEMENT OF MR. JOHNNY ORAM, EXECUTIVE DIRECTOR, CHALDEAN ASSYRIAN BUSINESS ALLIANCE

Mr. ORAM. Thank you very much, Mr. Chairman, members, guests. My name is Johnny Oram. I am the executive director of the Chaldean Assyrian Business Alliance based in Detroit, Michigan. We are an organization that is aimed at fostering professional relationships and also to enhance the betterment of our societies globally, especially at a critical time when the existence of our peoples in our motherland as well as in Syria is being threatened.

Before I go into recommendations for this committee, I would like to talk briefly about our peoples' presence here in the United States. We the Assyrians, Chaldeans, and the Syriacs are the descendants of the original peoples of Abraham. We are the indigenous peoples of Iraq. We are defined by our language, which is Aramaic, the language that the Lord Jesus Christ spoke. Oldest language in the world. We are also defined by our faith. We are a part of the Eastern Rite of the Roman Catholic Church in union with Rome. A good number of our Assyrians are from the Assyrian Church of the East, the Ancient Church of the East, and the Syriac Church, as well as the Presbyterian, and many other denominations.

My people immigrated to the United States in the early 20th century to come to the greatest nation in the history on Earth, a land where they can seek opportunities and be free to profess their faith. They came to communities such as Detroit to seek employment in our automotive plants. They came to the United States not only because of economic opportunities, but they came to the United States because the church and we had communities here that they were attracted to. When you have a church, they will come. And, subsequently, there are schools, which I will elaborate here a little bit later, but that is very important to our communities: The faith and family.

Oftentimes, the Assyrians and the Chaldeans are categorized as Arabs. However, we are not Arabs, but rather, we are in predominantly Arab countries, though many of our people live in Iran and Turkey, which are not Arab countries. Again, we are the indigenous peoples of the land. Nineveh was the capital of Assyria afterall. We have close to 150,000 Chaldeans and Assyrians in the metro Detroit region alone and an additional 200,000 throughout the United States in Chicago, Phoenix, San Diego, San Jose, Turlock, and Modesto. We also have a significant Syriac community in New York and Connecticut.

My people here in the United States have a deep connection and a relationship to our persecuted refugees in Iraq and Syria. And we have welcomed thousands of them who have come to the United States with open arms. We feel for them.

I would like to touch point on the people who want to leave. So I am going to go ahead and kind of emphasize on that here. Seeing as Christians and other minorities are particularly targeted by the Islamic State, it is imperative that they be given special consideration in the search for asylum. This is amplified by the fact that they even face persecution in asylum and shelters in Europe by radicals. Nuri Kino, a world renowned investigative journalist and founder of the grassroots human rights organization A Demand for Action, has been instrumental in uncovering this in Sweden and other places throughout Europe. Our people are being harassed. Our people are being threatened. They are being intimidated. They are being coerced, even in Europe.

The opening of the new processing centers in Erbil and Beirut, where the majority of Christians flee from Iraq and Syria, were positive steps. But the number of people processed must be increased to deal with the overwhelming. As far assimilating into the United States, I think this is a perfect time to have a conversation and to talk about schools like Keys Grace Academy in Madison Heights, Michigan. I alluded to schools. This is a first of its kind in the Nation where they have engaged in Assyrian language immersion and basically preserving our identity and our culture. And the school has also helped kids adjust and integrate into American culture while maintaining their heritage in a meaningful way.

The public education system here in the United States is woefully unprepared to deal with these kids, many of them who have seen severe trauma. But schools, like Keys Grace Academy, which are run by our own Chaldean and Assyrian people, who understand what they have been through, are extremely critical. Furthermore, groups like the Chaldean Community Foundation in Sterling Heights, Michigan—basically it is a suburb of Detroit. This organization has been instrumental in helping Assyrian and Chaldean refugees to assimilate into American society. The foundation processes over 20,000 visitors annually as they help our new arrivals into the metro Detroit region seek employment, health care, assistance, education, moral support, and so on. Our community in metro Detroit is 150,000 strong and growing. As you are all aware, Mr. Chairman, members and guests, my Congressman from Michigan's 11th congressional district, David Trott, offered an amendment to the NDAA, the National Defense Authorization Act, that passed the House on May 17, which is aimed at protecting Christians and other religious minorities throughout the Middle East from the Islamic State-led genocide by establishing a U.N. refugee processing center in Erbil. This requires the United Nations to step up and do its share to protect our vulnerable communities in Iraq, as well as the United Nations.

I also urge the United States Congress to reform the Refugee Act of 1980 by establishing more P-2 and P-3 visas for our refugees and bypassing the U.N.-mandated refugee allotments and quotas. Moreover, this is also going to be important for the refugees in that they can apply directly to admission to the United States of America, rather than be sent off to other lands, such as various designations in Europe and elsewhere, where they have been unwelcome.

Now, I would like to elaborate on the people who want to stay. The reality is that the vast majority of people will not be able or

desire to leave. So the particularly important measure will be with
those that deal with the situation in Iraq and Syria. In the short
term, emergency aid going directly to these organizations on the
ground is extremely critical. Aid organizations, like Help Iraq, the
Assyrian Aid Society, ACERO, the Syriac Patriarchate, et cetera,
have a proven ability to actually get aid to our people. Other organizations, such as my colleague Shachar Zahavi over at IsraAID,
Israel's leading humanitarian organization, have been instrumental
in providing aid, relief, and medical care for our refugees.

The fact that our people are still being targeted in UNHCR
camps by locals, not by U.N. staff, they almost exclusively stop
going to these U.N.-run camps and, therefore, critical aid doesn't
reach them through traditional channels. Our aid organizations,
which I have alluded to earlier, fill in the void as much as possible.
But resources are always in dire straits. We have seen some legislative support in the Senate's foreign operations appropriations.
But, unfortunately, the legislative support has not translated to
enough material support on the ground.

I can't really emphasize how important this is, but we must directly support our indigenous aid organizations on the ground. For
example, our own USAID sends funds to the United Nations with
the intent of distributing these funds to our communities in Iraq
and Syria. The Iraqi and Syrian Christians are not receiving any
of these moneys. All this money goes to the UNHCR camps, a place
which is unsafe for Christians and Yazidis and other religious minorities. Where is the security apparatus to protect our people in
these camps, especially when they are trying to receive critical aid
for their very own survival? Supporting local security forces in Iraq
and Syria is the best way to ensure a stable environment where
people are able to return. After the Islamic State invaded, both the
Peshmerga and the Iraqi Army abandoned Christian and Yazidi
areas of the Nineveh Plains and Sinjar, leaving the inhabitants defenseless and deeply distrustful of the institutional security apparatus.

Support authorized through the NDAA for the Assyrian,
Chaldean, Syriac Christians, and other minorities in Iraq and
Syria is crucial in standing up to these forces.

I worked with A Demand For Action on these efforts, and there
has been some support realized for Syriac Assyrian forces in Syria,
but the forces in Iraq are going to need considerable support. But
it is support that they deserve and that they are entitled to and
is the only way to gain confidence of the people who have inhabited
these lands for thousands of years.

Finally, the creation of a safe haven with international protection
which ultimately would be transitional to a province in the
Nineveh Plains with the semblance of self-governance and self-se-
curity is the only way to regain the trust of the minorities who feel
that they were betrayed by the Iraqi Government and the KRG.

These issues affecting our communities in Iraq and Syria are especially addressed in H. Res. 440, a resolution introduced by Congressman David Trott and Congressman Sherman of California,
which calls for precise actions that can positively affect the situation on the ground. Marking up that resolution is critical as it
would additionally serve as a moral boon to the beleaguered people

as it is the first resolution in congressional history to recognize the Simele massacre in 1933, an event where 3,000 Assyrians were massacred under the watch of the Iraqi Government.

I would like to talk on the IDP situation in Turkey. Sixty-seven years ago, right here in Washington, DC, all the signatories to the North Atlantic Treaty Organization, NATO, agreed to the following: The parties to this treaty reaffirm their faith in the purposes and principles of the Charter of the United Nations and their desire to live in peace with all peoples and all governments. They are determined to safeguard the freedom, the common heritage, and the civilization of their peoples, founded on the principles of democracy, individual liberty, and the rule of law. They seek to promote stability and well-being in the North Atlantic area. They are resolved to unite their efforts for collective defense and for the preservation of peace and security.

Mr. Chairman, Members, being a member of NATO requires respecting peoples of all religions and all faiths. Many of our churches in Turkey are being confiscated by President Erdogan and the Council of Ministers in Turkey under this whole guise that they are basically going to reform and revitalize those communities that have been impacted by war, especially in places like Diyarbakir. My very bishop, Francis Kalabat, in Detroit, Michigan, and many Assyrian and Chaldean clergy oftentimes have to travel to Turkey to administer to the faithful there because our faithful basically cannot profess their faith freely.

This is a NATO ally. This is basically a campaign to begin the extermination of Christianity in the Middle East, and that really doesn't bode well for us. This is of extremely vital importance to our national security and to the security of the world. These include Catholics, Protestants, and Orthodox churches that date close to 2,000 years.

Mr. Chairman, I would sincerely request that you and your colleagues move forward existing efforts in Congress to urge the Turkish Government, led by President Erdogan and his Council of Ministers, to immediately return these churches to their rightful owners. This right here is an example of continued persecution and displacement of Christians in the region. Again, Turkey is supposed to be our ally, but they are not being a good actor in the situation. These actions clearly undermine the very agreement that the Turkish Government signed to become a member of NATO in 1952.

We, the United States of America, have a moral and fundamental obligation. We need to step up as leaders of the free world and help the thousands of Christians and other religious minorities escape displacement and death, give them hope when they have lost hope, and to reassure them that they have a place that they can come to if they so choose where they can be a part of a nation and contribute to our economy and our society.

As I have mentioned earlier, we have the resources to absorb them. This is the right thing to do. Thank you very much, Mr. Chairman. May God bless you and God bless America.

[The prepared statement of Mr. Oram follows:]

Next Steps: The post genocide recognition steps involve both immigration and repatriation efforts.

Thank you Mr. Chairman, Members and Guests,

My name is Johnny Oram, Executive Director of the Chaldean Assyrian Business Alliance of Detroit, Michigan. We are a group that is aimed at promoting professional and social causes important to our communities worldwide, especially at a critical time where the existence of our people in our Mother Land of Iraq is being threatened.

Before I go into recommendations for this Committee, I'd like to talk briefly about our people's presence in these United States. We Assyrians/Chaldeans/Syriacs are the descendants of the original peoples of Abraham. We are defined by our language, Aramaic, which is the language in which our Lord Jesus Christ spoke. We are also defined by your Faith, as we are an Eastern Rite of the Roman Catholic Church. A good number of Assyrians are from the Assyrian Church of the East, the Ancient Church of the East, the Syriac Church, as well as Presbyterian, etc. My people immigrated to the United States in the early 20th Century, to come to the greatest country in history, a land where they can seek opportunity and be free to profess their faith. Oftentimes the Assyrians and Chaldeans are categorized as Arabs, however, we are not Arabs but rather we live in predominantly Arab countries, though many live in Iran and Turkey which are not Arab countries. We are the indigenous peoples to that land, Nineveh was the capital of Assyria after all. We have close to 150,000 Chaldeans/Assyrians in the Metro Detroit region alone and additional 200,000 throughout the United States, in Chicago, Phoenix, San Diego, San Jose, Modesto, Turlock as well as in the large Syriac communities in New York and Connecticut. My people here in the United States have a deep connection and relationship to our persecuted refugees and we have welcomed thousands of those have come to the United States with open arms. We feel for them!

People who want to leave: Seeing as Christians and other minorities are particularly targeted by ISIS it is imperative that they be given special consideration in their search for asylum. This is amplified by the fact that they even face persecution in asylum shelters in Europe by radicals. Nuri Kino, a world renowned investigative journalist and founder of the grassroots human rights group A Demand For Action has been instrumental in uncovering this in Sweden and elsewhere. The opening of new processing center in Erbil and Beirut, where the majority of Christians flee from Iraq and Syria, were a positive step but the number of people processed must be increased to deal with the overwhelming. As far as assimilating into the US, I think this is a perfect time to talk about schools like KEYS Grace Academy and how they help kids adjust and integrate into American culture while maintaining their heritage in a meaningful way. The public education system is woefully unprepared to deal with these kids, many of whom have severe trauma, but schools like KEYS which are run by our own people who understand what they've been through are critical. Furthermore, groups like the Chaldean Community Foundation in Sterling Heights, Michigan, a suburb of Detroit, have been instrumental in helping Assyrian and Chaldean refugees to assimilate into American society. The Foundation sees over 20,000 visitors annually as they help our new arrivals to learn English, find work, seek health care, and employment. Our community in Metro Detroit is 150,000 strong and growing.

As you are all aware, my Congressman from Michigan's 11th District, Dave Trott offered an amendment to the NDAA (National Defense Authorization Act) that passed the House on May 17th, which is aimed at protecting Christians and other religious minorities throughout the Middle East from the IS led genocide by establishing a UN Refugee Processing Center in Erbil. This requires the United Nations to step up and do its share to protecting our vulnerable communities in Iraq. I also urge the United States Congress to reform the Refugee Act of 1980 by establishing more P2/P3 visas for our refugees and bypassing the UN mandated refugee allotments / quotas. Moreover, this is also going to be important for the refugees in that they can apply directly for admission to the United States rather than be sent off to other lands such as various destinations in Europe and elsewhere.

People who want to stay: The reality is the vast majority of people will not be able or desire to leave, so the particularly important measures will those that deal with the situation in Iraq and Syria. In the short term, emergency aid going directly to the organizations on the ground is critical. Aid organizations like Help Iraq, ACERO, Syriac Patriarchate, etc have a proven ability to actually get aid to our people. The fact that our people are still being targeted in UNHCR camps (by locals, not UNHCR itself) they almost exclusively stopped going to UN runs camps and therefore critical aid doesn't reach them through the traditional channels. Our aid orgs fill the void as much as possible but resources are always in dire straits. We've seen some legislative support in SFOPS appropriations, but unfortunately the legislative support has not translated into enough material support on the ground. We MUST directly support our indigenous aid organizations on the ground. For example, our own USAID sends funds to the United Nations with the intent of distributing these funds to our communities in Iraq / Syria. The Iraqi and Syrian Christians are not receiving these very funds. All this money goes to the UNHCR camps, a place that is unsafe for Christians and Yezidis. Where is the security apparatus to protect our people in these camps, especially when they are trying to receive critical aid for their survival?

Supporting local security forces in Iraq and Syria is the best way to ensure a stable environment where people are able to return. After ISIS invaded, both the Peshmerga and Iraqi army abandoned the Christian and Yazidi areas of the Nineveh Plains and Sinjar, leaving the inhabitants defenseless and deeply distrustful of the institutional security apparatus. Support authorized through the NDAA for Assyrian/Chaldean/Syriac Christians and other minorities in Iraq and Syria is crucial to standing up these forces. You worked with A Demand For Action on these efforts, and there has been some support realized for Syriac/Assyrian forces in Syria, but the forces in Iraq are going to need considerable support, but it is support they deserve and are entitled to and is the only way to gain the confidence of the people who have inhabited that land since time immemorial.

Finally, the creation of a Safe Haven with international protection, which ultimately would be transitioned to a province in the Nineveh Plains with some semblance of self governance and self security is the only way to regain the trust of the minorities who feel they were betrayed by the Iraqi government and the KRG.

These issues affecting our communities in Iraq and Syria are specifically addressed in H.Res.440, a resolution introduced by Congressman Trott of Michigan and Congressman Sherman of California which calls for precise actions that can positively affect the situation on the ground. Marking up that resolution is critical, as it would additionally serve as a moral boon to our beleaguered people as it is the first resolution in Congressional history to recognize the Simele Massacre of 1933.

IDP's in Turkey

67 year ago here right here in Washington, D.C, all the signatories to the North Atlantic Treaty Organization (NATO) agreed to the following: "The Parties to this Treaty reaffirm their faith in the purposes and principles of the Charter of the United Nations and their desire to live in peace with all peoples and all governments. They are determined to safeguard the freedom, common heritage and civilization of their peoples, founded on the principles of democracy, individual liberty and the rule of law. They seek to promote stability and well-being in the North Atlantic area. They are resolved to unite their efforts for collective defence and for the preservation of peace and security." Being a member of NATO requires respecting of peoples of all faiths. Many of our Churches in Turkey are being confiscated. My Bishop, Francis Kallabat and other Assyrian, Chaldean, and Syriac clergy oftentimes have to travel to Turkey to administer to our faithful there because Turkey has seized many Churches and deemed them as state property. These include Catholic, Protestant, and Orthodox churches that date close to 2000 years. Mr. Chairman, I would sincerely request that you and your colleagues to move forward in existing efforts in this Congress to urge the Turkish government led by President Erdogan and his Council of Ministers to immediately return these Churches to their rightful owners. This right here is an example of the continued persecution and displacement of Christians in the region. Isn't Turkey supposed to be our ally? These actions clearly undermine the very agreement that the Turkish government signed to become of a member of our NATO alliance in 1952.

We have a moral obligation here to step up as the leader of the Free World and help the thousands of Christians and other religious minorities escape displacement and death, give them hope when they have lost it, and to reassure them that they have a place that they can come to if they so choose, where they can be a part of our nation and contribute to American society. As I had mentioned earlier, we have the resources to absorb them. This is the right thing to do.

I thank you very much. God Bless you all and May God Bless America.

Mr. SMITH. Thank you so much, Mr. Oram, for your testimony and recommendations and insights.

I would like to now recognize Ms. Naomi Kikoler, and thank you for being here.

STATEMENT OF MS. NAOMI KIKOLER, DEPUTY DIRECTOR, SIMON-SKJODT CENTER FOR THE PREVENTION OF GENOCIDE, UNITED STATES HOLOCAUST MEMORIAL MUSEUM

Ms. KIKOLER. Thank you, Chairman Smith and Ranking Member Bass, for holding a hearing on this important issue and for the opportunity to testify. I ask that you include in the record the text of the Holocaust Memorial Museum's report issued last November, entitled "Our Generation is Gone: The Islamic State's Targeting of Iraqi Minorities in Ninewa."

Last month, I was sitting with a Yazidi woman in a displaced persons camp outside of Dohuk in the Kurdistan region of Iraq. She was kidnapped by Islamic State fighters in the village of Kocho during an attack where hundreds of Yazidi men were killed. When I met her, she, along with her two young children, had escaped her Islamic State captor in Syria only 2 weeks earlier. She had been forcibly converted to Islam, and for almost 2 years, she was held as a sex slave. She and her children are the face of a modern day genocide that is being perpetrated by the Islamic State. For those still being held today, that genocide is ongoing.

The administration's determination that this self-proclaimed Islamic State committed genocide and crimes against humanity against religious minorities is an important recognition of the heinous crimes committed by the Islamic State and the suffering of victims like the woman I met and her children.

However, if the label of genocide is truly to have meaning for the victims of that crime, then this discussion should evolve from a question of what happened to how to protect vulnerable communities, using military and nonmilitary tools, from future threats by the Islamic State and other extremist groups. This includes how to secure justice and accountability for the victims of their crimes.

Genocide is a rare occurrence. There is no blueprint for how the United States Government responds in situations where genocide has been committed or is taking place. With this in mind, we at the Simon-Skjodt Center for the Prevention of Genocide traveled last month to the Kurdistan region of Iraq and to newly liberated areas by Mount Sinjar to assess what needs to be done to protect vulnerable minorities as a followup to the report released in November 2015 documenting the commission of genocide, crimes against humanity, and ethnic cleansing committed by the Islamic State against minorities.

Our trip starkly revealed that these communities remain at risk of future atrocities. Those who stay in exile in the Kurdistan region of Iraq are physically safe, yet they yearn to return home. As long as the Islamic State exists, these communities will remain vulnerable. The Islamic State still occupies large swaths of land in Nineveh, making it impossible for minority communities to return home.

Certain liberated areas are also too dangerous for civilians to return home as they are within the range of ISIS mortar fire. This is particularly true for communities on the south side of Mount Sinjar and those close to Mosul.

Defeating the Islamic State, therefore, should remain a key priority of the U.S. Government's efforts if our hope is to ensure the very survival of these communities. Yet to animate this objective, civilian protection and the prevention of atrocity should be at the core of that strategy. We know from past cases that this requires a comprehensive and sustained strategy using military and non-military tools that is calibrated to respond to evolving conditions on the ground to prevent genocide and other mass atrocities. In this context, a strategy would include day-after planning to identify scenarios and tools that would mitigate potential future flashpoints and implement strategies to address them, including rebuilding liberated areas, promoting reconciliation between groups, advancing justice and accountability efforts, and securing a political resolution between the Government of Iraq and the Kurdish Regional Government to the disputed areas in which many of Iraq's minorities live.

The most common sentiment that we heard from displaced minority communities and one that needs to be addressed is their lack of trust in the officials and institutions that are responsible for their physical protection and for guaranteeing their legal rights, as well as their deep distrust of their former Sunni Arab neighbors who they perceive as having been complicit in ISIS' attacks.

Religious minorities continue to feel that the Iraqi security forces and the Kurdish Peshmerga abandoned them when the Islamic State attacked Nineveh. Many also continue to feel that they are being used as political pawns by the Government of Iraq and the Kurdish Regional Government in the ongoing contest over the disputed areas. This leaves them nervous about who and how their land will be administered should they return home.

For over 10 years, religious minorities were targeted on the basis of their identity by extremist groups and were politically marginalized. The early warning of their vulnerabilities went largely unheeded, and as a result, many saw fleeing the country as their only protection option. Today, in the absence of what they, again, see as being credible actors to provide their physical protection, many communities are seeking to arm themselves. New threats are also emerging for not just religious minorities but also for the Sunni Arab population who may be the victims of revenge killings. The proliferation of unregulated and poorly trained militias may pose additional threats to civilians in areas liberated from the Islamic State as they seek to liberate additional territory. Many that we interviewed expressed concerns about the potential for conflict between militias within particular religious communities and amongst religious groups.

This all underscores that defeating the Islamic State and protecting vulnerable communities requires more than just a military strategy if civilians are to be protected. It requires tackling the root causes that allowed the Islamic State to rise and that enhance the vulnerabilities of minority communities.

In light of this, we believe that there are four principle areas where additional efforts could be paid to ensure both the immediate protection needs of vulnerable communities seeking to return home and ensure that the long-term and systematic drivers of conflict are mitigated.

Those are, first, an explicit policy to provide genuine physical protection to vulnerable populations. Protection could include strategies for employing local, domestic, and international actors to provide security to ethnic and religious minorities returning to liberated lands and Sunni Arab populations at risk of reprisal killings.

In planning military operations and broader policy objectives, actors should consider the possible unintended consequences of the actions taken and whether they will heighten risks for civilian populations living under the Islamic State's control and/or might contribute to future cycles of violence.

The Iraqi Government and international donors should ensure that all Iraqi security forces, Iraqi Kurdish Peshmerga, and local militias fully adhere to international human rights and humanitarian law standards and are held accountable for violations in accordance with international standards. Withholding military assistance to those groups who do not adhere to these standards could be a powerful tool in addressing the behavior of bad actors.

Second is support for stabilization and reconstruction efforts in liberated areas. This includes increasing the presence of development assistance from relevant agencies and departments. Many of the displaced expressed concerns to us that they will be unable to return home in the absence of economic opportunity and the reconstruction of their devastated region. High rates of unemployment within the Sunni population and perceived economic inequity was one of drivers of the rise of the Islamic State. Affected regions must be rebuilt and the engagement of the international community must be sustained in that endeavor in the years to come.

A critical component of stabilization and reconstruction efforts is investing in reconciliation so that diverse communities can once again live alongside each other. In the absence of such efforts, there is a grave potential for future conflict between communities.

Third, transitional justice efforts are central to responding to the commission of past crimes and the deterrence of future crimes. The clearest obligation in the Convention on the Prevention and Punishment of the Crime of Genocide is to punish the perpetrators of genocide, and international justice is the cornerstone upon which the international community has responded to the crime of genocide, from Nuremberg 70 years ago to the international criminal tribunals for Rwanda, Yugoslavia, and Cambodia.

Today, substantial support is needed to investigate, collect, and analyze evidence; secure mass grave sites; and detain perpetrators for the purpose of future prosecution. In this effort, we can't lose sight of the importance of holding individuals accountable for crimes committed at the local level.

The most common answer to the question of how can trust be built between minorities and the Sunni Arab population that we pose to people who are displaced was that those who committed crimes in their towns and villages needed to be held accountable in a court. The rampant culture of impunity has left high levels of distrust amongst ordinary Iraqis. They need to see justice advanced not only against the Islamic State's leaders for genocide but also for the crimes committed by their neighbors in their very own communities. This necessitates detaining fighters, investigating their crimes, and then prosecuting them at the national as well as possibly the international level.

Fourth is securing the political resolution to the ongoing dispute between the Kurdish Regional Government and the Iraqi Government over Nineveh. Our report was very clear in identifying the ongoing dispute as a key factor that exacerbated the vulnerability of minority communities in part because the dispute is perceived as having contributed to growing support for extremist groups, and when the Islamic State advanced, there were no clear lines of responsibility. As long as responsibility for protecting these communities remains in question, vulnerabilities will remain acute and create a vacuum that the Islamic State or a successor group could exploit.

Finally, to recognize a genocide has happened is to acknowledge a collective failure to prevent the crime of all crimes and to uphold the commitment to never again. Going forward, the U.S. and other governments will need to place civilian protection and the prevention of atrocities at the core of their counter-ISIL strategies, but the commitment to prevent and protect minorities must extend beyond the current threat posed by the Islamic State. We must endeavor to ensure that in 10 years, we are not yet again meeting in the wake of another failure to protect vulnerable minorities in Iraq and Syria.

Countering the Islamic State and preventing future atrocities perpetrated by other groups necessitates an ongoing assessment of those groups' motivations, organization, and capabilities for committing atrocity crimes, and of the vulnerabilities of at-risk communities. Continuous monitoring and analysis of the warning signs and risk indicators on the ground will be needed and strategies developed to ensure that threats facing minorities in the future are mitigated.

That is what upholding the commitment to prevent, enshrined in the Genocide Convention, should mean. Thank you.

[The prepared statement of Ms. Kikoler follows:]

Naomi Kikoler
Deputy Director, Simon Skjodt Center for the Prevention of Genocide
Committee on Foreign Affairs, Subcommittee on Africa, Global Health, Global Human Rights, and International Organizations
May 26, 2015, The ISIS Genocide Declaration: What Next?

Thank you, Chairman Smith and Ranking Member Bass for holding a hearing on this important issue and for your role in raising the profile of the situation facing civilians in northern Iraq. I ask that you include with my written statement the text of the Holocaust Museum report issued last November "Our Generation is Gone: The Islamic State's Targeting of Iraqi Minorities in Ninewa."

Last month I was sitting with a Yezidi woman in a displaced persons camp outside Dohuk, in the Kurdistan Region of Iraq. She was kidnapped by Islamic State (IS) fighters in the village of Kocho during an attack where almost every Yezidi man they captured was massacred. When I met her she, along with her two young children, had escaped her IS captor in Syria only two weeks earlier. She had been forcibly converted to Islam and for almost two years she was held as a sex slave. She, and her children, are the face of a modern-day genocide that is being perpetrated by the Islamic State. For those still being held today, that genocide is ongoing.

The Administration's determination that the self-proclaimed Islamic State committed genocide and crimes against humanity against religious minorities is an important recognition of the heinous crimes committed by IS and the suffering of victims like the woman I met and her children.

However, if the label of genocide is truly going to have meaning for the victims of that crime then this discussion should evolve from a question of what happened, to how to protect vulnerable communities using military and non-military tools from future threats by IS and other extremist groups, this includes how to secure justice and accountability for the victims of their crimes.

Genocide is a rare occurrence. There is no blue print for how the US government responds in situations where genocide has been committed, or is taking place. With this in mind, we at the Simon-Skjodt Center for the Prevention of Genocide travelled last month to the Kurdistan Region of Iraq, and to newly liberated areas by Mount Sinjar to assess what needs to be done to protect vulnerable minorities as a follow-up to the report we released in November 2015 documenting the commission of genocide, crimes against humanity and ethnic cleansing committed by IS against minorities. We met with displaced communities, religious leaders, security forces, civil society and Kurdish regional government and coalition officials.

Our trip starkly revealed that these communities remain at risk of future atrocities. Those who stay in exile in the Kurdistan Region of Iraq are physically safe yet they yearn to return home. Should they seek to return home to areas not liberated from IS they face the risk of atrocities, while new threats and vulnerabilities to minorities and other civilians are also emerging.

As long as the Islamic State exists, these communities will remain vulnerable. IS still occupies large swaths of land in Ninewa making it impossible for minority communities to return home. Certain liberated areas are also too dangerous for civilians to return home as they are within the range of IS mortar fire. This is particularly true for communities on the south side of Mount Sinjar and those close to Mosul.

Defeating IS therefore should remain a key priority for the US government if our hope is to ensure the survival of these communities. To animate this objective, civilian protection and the prevention of atrocities should be at the core of the strategy.

We know, from past cases, that this requires a comprehensive and sustained strategy using military and non-military tools that is calibrated to respond to evolving conditions on the ground, to prevent genocide and other mass atrocities. In this context, a strategy would include 'day-after' planning to identify scenarios and tools that would mitigate potential future flashpoints and implement strategies to address them: including rebuilding liberated areas; promoting reconciliation between groups; advancing justice and accountability efforts; and securing a political resolution between the Government of Iraq and the Kurdish Regional Government to the disputed areas in which many of Iraq's minorities live.

The most common sentiment that we heard from displaced minority communities, and that needs to be addressed, is their lack of trust in the officials and institutions that are responsible for their physical protection and for guaranteeing their legal rights, as well as their distrust of their former Sunni Arab neighbours who they perceive as having been complicit in IS' attacks. Religious minorities continue to feel little trust towards the Iraqi Security Forces and Kurdish Peshmerga who they feel abandoned them when IS attacked Ninewa. Many also continued to feel that they are being used as political pawns by the government of Iraq, and the Kurdish regional government, in the ongoing contest over the disputed areas, this leaves them nervous about who and how their land will be administered should they return home.

For over ten years religious minorities were targeted, on the basis of their identity, by extremists groups and were politically marginalized. Little was done to protect them physically or legally, and many saw their only protection option being to flee Iraq. Today, minorities often express concern that IS is only the latest iteration of that phenomenon and that in its wake a new extremist group will emerge and target them again. Thus, in the absence of what they see as being credible actors to provide for their physical protection, many communities are seeking to arm themselves.

New threats are also emerging for not just religious minorities, but also for the Sunni Arab population. The proliferation of unregulated, poorly trained religious militias may pose additional threats to civilians in areas liberated from ISIS, and as they seek to liberate additional territory. Many that we interviewed expressed concerns about the potential for conflict between militias within particular religious communities, and amongst religious groups.

There is the potential that Sunni Arabs, some of whom face threats from ISIS, may also be the victims of revenge killings and displacement. We were repeatedly told by religious minorities that they could not trust their former Sunni Arab neighbours and that Sunni Arabs could not return to their former homes in Ninewa, if they did, they will be killed

This underscores that defeating ISIL and protecting vulnerable communities will require more than a military strategy if civilians are to be protected from a recurrence of atrocities. It requires tackling the conditions that allowed IS to rise, and that enhanced the vulnerabilities of minority communities. Many of those conditions and vulnerabilities, including weak rule of law, a culture of impunity, sectarianism, gaps in minorities legal protection and political marginalization, lack of trust, and the ongoing territorial dispute over parts of Ninewa between the governments in Baghdad and Erbil, remain today.

Going Forward:

In recognition of this, we believe that there are four principal areas where additional effort could be paid to ensure both the immediate protection needs of vulnerable communities seeking to return home and that the long term and systemic drivers of conflict are mitigated:

Those are:

First, an explicit policy to provide genuine physical protection to vulnerable populations. Protection could include strategies for employing local, domestic, and international actors to provide security to ethnic and religious minorities returning to liberated lands and Sunni-Arab populations at risk of reprisal killings.

In planning military operations and broader policy objectives, actors should consider the possible unintended consequences of the actions taken and whether they will heighten risks for civilian populations living under IS control, and/or might contribute to future cycles of violence. The Iraqi government and international donors should ensure that all Iraqi security forces, Iraqi Kurdish Peshmerga, and local militias fully adhere to international human rights and humanitarian law standards and are held accountable for violations in accordance with international standards. Withholding military assistance to those groups who do not adhere to these standards could be a powerful tool in addressing the behavior of any bad actors.

Second, is support for stabilization and reconstruction efforts in liberated areas. This includes increasing the presence of development assistance of relevant agencies/departments. Many of the displaced expressed concerns that they will be unable to return home in the absence of economic opportunity and reconstruction of their devastated region. High rates of unemployment within the Sunni population and perceived economic inequity was a driver of the rise of IS. Affected regions must be rebuilt and the engagement of the international community sustained in the years to come. A critical component of stabilization and reconstruction efforts is investing in reconciliation so that diverse communities can once again live alongside each other. In the absence of such efforts there is a grave potential for future conflict between communities.

Third, transitional justice efforts are central to responding the commission of past crimes and the deterrence of future crimes. The clearest obligation in the Convention on the Prevention and Punishment of the Crime of Genocide is to punish the perpetrators of genocide and international justice is the cornerstone upon which the international community has responded to the crime of genocide—from Nuremberg 70 years ago to the international criminal tribunals for Rwanda, Yugoslavia, and Cambodia. Today substantial support is needed to investigate, collect and analyze evidence, secure mass grave sites and detain perpetrators for the purpose of future prosecutions.

In this effort, we cannot loose sight of the importance of holding individuals accountable for crimes committed at the local level. The most common answer to the question of "how can trust be built between minorities and the Sunni Arab population" was that those who committed crimes in their towns and villages needed to be held accountable in a court. The rampant culture of impunity has left high levels of distrust amongst ordinary Iraqi's. They need to see justice advanced not only against IS' leaders for genocide, but also for the crimes committed by their neighbours in their own communities. This necessitates detaining fighters, investigating their crimes, and then prosecuting them at the national, as well as possibly the international level.

Fourth, is securing a political resolution to the ongoing dispute between the Kurdish Regional Government and the Iraqi central government over the Ninewa plain. Our report was very clear in identifying the ongoing dispute as a key factor that exacerbated the vulnerability of minority communities, in part because the dispute is perceived as having contributed to growing support for extremist groups and when ISIS advanced there were no clear lines of responsibility. As long as responsibility for protecting these communities remains in question vulnerabilities will remain acute and create a vacuum that IS or a successor group could again exploit.

Finally, to recognize that genocide has happened is to acknowledge a collective failure to prevent the crime of all crimes and uphold the commitment to 'Never Again.' Going forward the US and other governments will need to place civilian protection and the prevention of atrocities at the core of their counter-ISIL strategies. But the commitment to prevent and protect minorities must extend beyond the current threat posed by IS. We must endeavor to ensure that in ten years we are not yet again meeting in the wake of another failure to protect vulnerable minorities in Iraq and Syria. Countering IS and preventing future atrocities perpetrated by other groups, necessitates an ongoing assessment of their motivations, organization, and capabilities for committing atrocity crimes, and of vulnerabilities of at-risk communities. Continuous monitoring and analysis of the warning signs and risk indicators on the ground will be needed and strategies developed to ensure that threats facing Minorities in the future are mitigated. This is what upholding the commitment to prevent, enshrined in the genocide convention, should mean.

———————

Mr. SMITH. Thank you so very much for your testimony and for reminding us of what the face of genocide is with your experience with the young woman and her two children. As you pointed out, she was forcibly converted to Islam. For almost 2 years, she was held as a sex slave. That is just numbing in how awful and horrific that reality has been, so thankfully you were there, and now you have conveyed that message to all of us. And that should be fresh impetus for all of us to do even more.

I would like to now yield to Mr. Crane, a former chief prosecutor of the Special Court for Sierra Leone.

STATEMENT OF MR. DAVID M. CRANE, PROFESSOR OF PRAC- TICE, SYRACUSE UNIVERSITY COLLEGE OF LAW (FORMER CHIEF PROSECUTOR, UNITED NATIONS SPECIAL COURT FOR SIERRA LEONE)

Mr. CRANE. Thank you, Mr. Chairman.

I want to thank the subcommittee, its staff and, in particular, its chairman for its decades-long fight against the atrocities committed by state and nonstate actors around the world. In fact, you and I have been working together since 2002, along with many members of this committee, in seeking justice for the oppressed.

We are in an age of extremes with adversaries never contemplated facing challenges that are most likely not solvable. The 21st century is shaping up to be no better than what I call the bloody 20th century, where over 225 million people died of nonnatural causes, over 100 million of which that I estimate at the hands of their own governments.

In the 21st century, conflict will be kaleidoscopic and dirty, with one or all sides ignoring international law. Our current planning in the United States and preparation cycle make us incapable of dealing with these kaleidoscopic conflicts and events, and I am working with the International Peace and Security Institute to quantify that data.

Despite this, we have seen the evolution of modern international criminal law, which has now given us the practical and legal capability of holding dictators, thugs, and their henchmen accountable for atrocity if there is a political will to do so. I underscore ''if there is a political will to do so.'' If we do have that political will, we have the experience now to prosecute those who feed on their own peoples.

Now, we have mentioned many numbers this afternoon related to casualties: 300,000 persons killed, over 10 million refugees moving about the region with no hope and no homes. But I do want to underscore that these are about human beings, individual human beings. When I was in Sierra Leone, I would hold townhall meetings, and I was in Makeni, the headquarters of the infamous Revolutionary United Front, who cut hands off of victims and other body parts. And as I was holding this townhall meeting, a young child soldier stood up. He was about 12, and he looked at me in the eye, and he began to weep, and he said: I killed people. I am sorry. I didn't mean it.

And as I was holding him in my arms as he wept, a young woman stood up 10 feet from me, most of her face was missing because it had been put in a pot of boiling water. She was holding her child, and she, through cracked lips, said: Seek justice.

That is why we do this. And that is why I want to underscore in my remarks today that we don't forget that it is individual human beings, one person at a time.

There has been a complete breakdown of the rule of law and accountability in the Levant. The laws of armed conflict are ignored, resulting in mounting civilian casualties. There is an increased use of banned weapons systems, such as barrel bombs and chemical weapons, along with the increase in various torture and execution methods not seen since the Dark Ages. The Caesar Report, which I coauthored and which we testified a year or so ago, found direct and clear and convincing evidence of this horror.

In the Levant region, there are three international crimes that are being committed. They have been highlighted in this testimony and are well-known by this subcommittee: War crimes, crimes against humanity, and possibly genocide. I want to underscore and caution that we have to be very careful that politicians and diplomats tend to rank or tier international crimes and holding out genocide as the top tier.

Well, I would just submit respectfully to this subcommittee that 300,000 people killed as a result of an international crime don't care whether it is a genocide, crime against humanity, or war crime. So I want to caution our use of terms. They are important, but they are crimes, and I also want to point out, of these three crimes, one is a specific intent crime, which means that you have to have a specific intent to destroy in whole or in part a peoples.

It is a difficult crime to prove, and in some cases, you almost need a smoking gun, so I would just caution this subcommittee, when they are considering the war crimes, watch out for tiering and ranking the crimes, as well as understanding that genocide, even though a very serious crime indeed, a crime of crimes, is a difficult and very specific type of crime, which at the legal level, has to be clearly or beyond a reasonable doubt proven each and every element.

So what is next then? You asked me that question. First, there must be a realization that the ISIS phenomenon is a decades-long challenge. We are entering into an effort that is of cold war ramifications.

At this time, we do not have a solution for this challenge. Until we do have a realistic and practical solution, we must understand that we may not be able to restore international peace and security, only manage some sense of security in the Levant. The conflict there truly is kaleidoscopic in nature, where if one thing changes, everything changes. We cannot predict or plan what happens next.

The cornerstone to a possible beginning of a solution is Arab resolve and cooperation. However, this may not be possible given political realities. The West cannot be seen as an interloper, only as a patient enabler and a facilitator. We can't be seen as launching the seventh crusade, so to speak.

Over the next several years, you must contain the ISIS threat regionally, stamp out ISIS' attempts to further their cause elsewhere and focus on achievable programs in the region locally and domestically, and I would underscore some of the important points made by my colleagues this afternoon.

I just would like to say a young man or woman who has a job and some hope for a better future is less likely to turn to terror and to ISIS. Essentially, what I am saying is that we cannot defeat ISIS using kinetic energy alone. In reality, it can only be done through economic revitalization, almost a Marshall Plan for the Middle East. It is that kind of commitment.

Additionally, we can take realistic steps to start an accountability mechanism for the region, particularly as it relates to ISIS atrocities. If we have the political will, we can establish some tried and true methods. We should start with a truth commission, not a reconciliation commission at this point, but start with a truth commission. Let's get something started. Let's get something going.

We also have the ability and the experience to set up a domestic court or an internationalized domestic court, even a hybrid regional court, which we did in the Special Court for Sierra Leone. The International Criminal Court, though an important and permanent entity, is politically, unfortunately, neutralized by the United Nations Security Council and, unfortunately, will not play a major part in this effort, even though we need to recognize that they do have a potential place. The practical reality is, a domestic court, an internationalized domestic court, or hybrid regional court supported by regional countries, countries in the region, is the most practical and realistic opportunity.

Now, these mechanisms can be headquartered in Iraq, Turkey, or Jordan, supported by members of the Arab League. The international community could assist and train commission or court personnel as requested and needed. The idea is having Arab states prosecuting Arabs for crimes against Arab peoples in violation of Arab laws.

Now, we have done this before with the Special Court for Sierra Leone. We have moved into an area, worked with peoples, developed methodologies, efficiently managed justice mechanisms and broad accountability to millions of victims there in West Africa. We have translated this success into the Syrian Accountability Project, where we have built a conflict map, a crime base matrix, sample indictments so that someday, when a domestic, regional, or international prosecutor is designated, we can hand this package over to them for their consideration to get things started.

So what are my conclusions? The Levant is an unmanageable space. International peace and security cannot be restored using today's outmoded problem-solving techniques. Thus, there are no foreseeable political or military solutions. This is a multifaceted, and I underscore, decades-long struggle. It is truly kaleidoscopic.

Our next step should be to continue to try and contain ISIS. On the periphery, create achievable regional and domestic programs, and I would humbly suggest perhaps that Marshall Plan.

Let's take away the reason for ISIS to be—no hope in the future. We have and can offer better alternatives, such as freedom and a jobs plan, possibly. It is within the realm of possibility to development a justice mechanism outside the U.N. Security Council. The focus should be using regional and domestic arrangements to create those mechanisms. We must not be discouraged. We must be patient and firm in our resolve for accountability, stability, and peace.

A little over 10 years ago, President Charles Taylor never thought that he would be held accountable for his crimes in West Africa, but today, he sits in a maximum security prison in Great Britain for the rest of his life paying the price for aiding and abetting the murder, rape, maiming, and mutilation of over 1.2 million human beings. We can hold ISIS accountable for their crimes and begin to establish some sense of peace in the Levant.

Thank you, Mr. Chairman, for this time. I stand ready to answer any questions.

[The prepared statement of Mr. Crane follows:]

Subcommittee on Africa, Global Health, Global

Human Rights, and International Organizations

Testimony of Dr. David M. Crane

26 May 2016

The ISIS Genocide Declaration: What Next?

Introduction

I want to thank this Subcommittee, its Staff, and in particular it's Chairman for the decade's long fight against the atrocities committed by state and non-state actors around the world.

I have been working with this Subcommittee since 2002 in that effort. It began while I was Chief Prosecutor of the international war crimes tribunal in West Africa called the Special Court for Sierra Leone. Over a period of three years, with the important bi-partisan support of this Subcommittee and the Foreign Affairs Committee, we were able to break up the blood diamond conspiracy; take down the most powerful warlord in Africa, President Charles Taylor; and build and manage an efficient justice mechanism that brought accountability to millions of victims there in West Africa.

I have been working on the tragedy of Syria and the Levant since the very beginning. In March 2011 I met with the Syrian National Congress to advise and to help them consider various justice mechanisms to hold those who committed atrocity in Syria. Through the Syrian Accountability Project at Syracuse University College of Law, which I founded, over the past five- plus years we have built a trial package that a domestic, regional or international prosecutor can consider in developing a case against all parties committing atrocity in the Levant. That package includes a conflict map, a crime base matrix, and other associated documents to include sample indictments. I used this very same technique in successfully prosecuting President Charles Taylor and his henchmen in West Africa.

Additionally, I came face to face with the beast of impunity in Syria when I investigated alleged torture of detainees as co-author of the Caesar Report which the House Foreign Affairs Committee held a hearing about a year or so ago.

We are in an age of extremes with adversaries never contemplated facing challenges that are most likely not solvable. The 21st Century is shaping up to be no better than the bloody 20th century where over 225 million people died of non-natural causes, over 100 million at the hands of their own governments. In the 21st Century conflict will be kaleidoscopic and dirty with one or all sides ignoring international law. Our current planning and preparation cycle makes us incapable of dealing with these kaleidoscopic events.

Despite this, we have seen the evolution of modern international criminal law which has now given us the practical and legal capability of holding dictators, thugs, and their henchmen accountable for atrocity, if there is a political will to do so. If there is that political will, we have the experience now to prosecute those who feed on their own peoples.

I will briefly answer the question--The ISIS Genocide Declaration: What Next? By briefly outlining the atrocities to date in the Levant, then focusing on the crimes there and committed by ISIS, followed by an answer to the extant question and then concluding with a few key "takeaways".

Atrocity in the Levant

Over 300,000 persons have been killed since 2011. Over 10 million refugees move about the region with no homes or future.

There is a complete breakdown of the rule of law and accountability. The laws of armed conflict are ignored resulting in mounting civilian casualties.

There is an increased use of banned weapons systems such as barrel bombs and chemical weapons, along with the increase in various torture and execution methods not seen since the Dark Ages.

The International Crimes Being Committed by ISIS

War Crimes

There is a body of international law and norms that protect those persons found on the battlefield and govern the types of weapons systems and how they are used through the principles of military necessity, proportionality, discrimination/distinction, and unnecessary suffering. A violation of these norms found mainly in the Geneva Conventions and The Hague Rules constitutes a war crime.

Crimes against Humanity

A catch-all category, a crime against humanity is a widespread and/or systematic attack on a civilian population usually by a government or an organized rebel group. No conflict is needed for a crime against humanity to happen.

Genocide?

The crime of genocide, enshrined in the Genocide Convention, is a specific criminal intent to destroy in whole or in part a peoples. This can be done through various means to include the destruction of the populace, their culture, religion, their art, literature, even their language.

Genocide is difficult to prove because of this specific intent. One almost needs a "smoking gun". Should there be a genocide the convention requires signatories to act to stop the crimes and to prosecute. This rarely happens in modern times.

It is not entirely clear at this time whether there is genocide in the Levant. Though it appears that genocide has begun it will take a proper investigation by a future court of tribunal to legally establish that case.

What is next?

First there must come a realization that the ISIS phenomenon is a decade's long challenge. At this time we do not have a solution for this challenge. Until we do have a realistic and practical solution we must understand that we may not be able to restore international peace and security only manage some sense of security in the Levant. The conflict there truly is kaleidoscopic where if one thing changes everything changes. We cannot predict or plan for what happens next.

The cornerstone to a possible beginning of a solution is Arab resolve and cooperation. However, this may not be possible given political realities. The West cannot be seen as an interloper, only as a patient enabler and facilitator. We can't be seen as launching the seventh crusade so to speak.

Over the next several years we must contain the ISIS threat regionally, stamp out ISIS attempts to further their cause elsewhere, and focus on achievable programs in the region, locally, and domestically. A young man or woman who has a job and some hope for a better future is less likely to turn to terror and to ISIS.

Essentially what I am saying is that we cannot defeat ISIS using kinetic energy alone. In reality it can only be done through economic revitalization...almost a Marshall Plan for the Middle East. A regional office managed by the International Monetary Fund (and the World Bank) could be the center point for this.

Additionally, we can take realistic steps to start an accountability mechanism for the region, particularly as it relates to ISIS atrocity. IF we have the political will we can establish:

A Truth Commission.

A domestic court or an internationalized domestic court.

A hybrid regional court.

These mechanisms can be headquartered in Iraq, Turkey, or Jordan supported by members of the Arab League. The international community could assist and train commission or court personnel as requested and needed. The ideal is having Arab states, prosecuting Arabs, for crimes against Arab peoples, in violation of Arab laws.

Conclusions

The Levant is an unmanageable space. International peace and security cannot be restored using today's outmoded problem solving technigues, thus there are no foreseeable political or military solutions. This is a multifaceted and decade's long struggle. It truly is kaleidoscopic.

Our next steps should be to continue to try and contain ISIS. On the periphery create achievable regional and domestic programs. Consider that Marshall Plan!

Let's take away the reason for ISIS to be...no hope in the future. We have and can offer a better alternative—freedom and jobs plan.

It is within the realm of possibility to develop justice mechanisms outside the UN Security Council realm. The focus should be using regional and domestic arrangements to create these mechanisms.

We must not be discouraged. We must be patient and firm in our resolve for accountability, stability, and peace. A little over ten years ago, President Charles Taylor never thought he would be held accountable for his crimes in West Africa, but today he sits in a maximum security prison in Great Britain for the rest of his life paying the price for aiding and abetting the murder, rape, maiming, and murder of over 1.2 million people. We can hold ISIS accountable for their crimes and begin to establish some sense of peace in the Levant. Thank you Mr. Chairman for this time. I stand ready to answer any questions.

Mr. SMITH. Thank you, Professor Crane, for your testimony, for your leadership. And one of the pictures that I will never forget is the picture that was all on the front pages or page 3 of most of the newspapers around the world of Charles Taylor receiving a 50-year prison sentence, eyes cast down, thinking, I am sure, that he would never be held to account for the atrocities he committed on the Liberian, Sierra Leonean, and other people of the region.

So thank you for that successful prosecution of the other men who committed such horrific acts of violence against innocent people, especially women and children, for that and for your recommendations. They are outstanding.

Just a few questions to start off. I will yield to my colleague, and then we will have perhaps a few more additional questions.

Mr. Anderson, you make a very strong point—Mr. Oram, you do it as well—that the aid that is meant to go to—or what many people think would get to Christians is not getting through and to other persecuted minorities, like the Yazidis, and the importance of backing indigenous efforts, particularly the churches, to get that aid through.

We had a hearing last—I chaired it with the Assistant Secretary Anne Richard under the auspices of the Helsinki Commission on why is it so many people went to flight and left and made their way into Europe? One is that there was gross underfunding of the international calls for subsistence.

Mr. Hamasaeed, you made the point as well that efforts continue to fall woefully short of the need for food, shelter, healthcare, education, and psychosocial support for those to deal with trauma in your testimony, and the number that we got was about 40 percent of the requests of the competent authorities, like the UNHCR, that is all they got. And this year, so far, we are at, for 2016, 23 percent funded, although we are not done, 2016. Forty percent, 42 percent, is, as you said, woefully, woefully underfunding.

One of biggest takeaways from that hearing came from the UNHCR representative, who said the reason why people left, one was the loss of hope; secondly, a cut to the World Food Programme of about 30 percent. And they said: That is it. They don't have our back. We are going to stagnate here, maybe even die. We are going to head to Europe or Germany or somewhere else where the pastures might be greener.

So the international community fatally, I think, underfunded those efforts. The U.S. led the effort. Perhaps we should have done more or mobilized more. This isn't a hearing to point fingers. It is to say: We have got to get it right. And my hope is that we will do a second hearing. Just so you know, Ms. Bass and I, we have already asked Rabbi Saperstein to come, the top point person for religious freedom. He couldn't come today, but he sends his regrets. He will make an appearance. We will also ask Anne Richard, Assistant Secretary at PRM, and others, because I do think there is a place where we need to be joined at the hip, congressional and executive branch, to make a difference in the lives of these people.

But the gross underfunding, and if you would elaborate a little bit on this 30-day window. Mr. Anderson, you talked about that if people don't get food and medicines—and any of you who would like to touch on this—they are literally at the point of starvation and, obviously, other terrible consequences from malnutrition.

Mr. ANDERSON. Well, I would say, Mr. Chairman, most of what we hear is anecdotal. Just this week, my assistant is in Erbil. I was speaking with him this morning, and he was calling me from a Yazidi camp. He told me that what he had been told was that the Yazidis in this camp had received one food drop from the U.N. when they arrived, and since that time, all of their assistance has come through the Archdiocese of Erbil. For example, all of their medical assistance comes through the medical clinic that we have been funding.

So if those sources stop, you can see here is a community, they are still living in tents. There is nothing available for them. So I would think maybe have the same kind of evidence that you are receiving, but we hear this from the religious leaders in Erbil, and we hear it from the religious leaders in Aleppo and throughout Syria. It is the same, same issue.

Mr. SMITH. Yes, Mr. Oram, and then Mr. Hamasaeed.

Mr. ORAM. Mr. Anderson, thank you. Yes, that is a common narrative in Erbil for our people. So, as I had mentioned in testimony, Mr. Chairman, organizations like Help Iraq, Assyrian Aid Society, ACERO, and others are basically doing the job of what governments and governmental agencies should be doing. And a lot of our people, a lot of this assistance goes to the U.N. and U.N.-run camps. But a lot of our Christians and other religious minorities are afraid to go to those camps because the—so one recommendation is to, really, in addition to the refugee processing center—we don't know—I know that there has been legislation to call for that and also to form some other—a venue for them to go and receive aid, so there needs to be a security apparatus in place, especially even at the U.N. camps, because most—a bulk of that aid goes to those camps.

Mr. SMITH. And you know, when I raise it with the UNHCR, as I did at that hearing and I have done ever since and before, they are very defensive, and I understand where they are coming from. It is not them. It is the people in the camp.

Mr. ORAM. Right.

Mr. SMITH. Those who wish them ill, "they" being the Christians or the Yazidis or the other minorities.

Mr. ORAM. That is correct. You are absolutely right.

Mr. SMITH. But that doesn't mean I don't have a responsibility and all of us to get the money, the food, and humanitarian assistance to those who are suffering.

Mr. ORAM. And that is why it is so extremely critical in, you know, the Senate's foreign operations appropriations mechanism to increase aid for these international nongovernmental organizations because they are preparing. So what oftentimes has happened is organizations like Help Iraq are vested with a responsibility of engaging in fundraising campaigns throughout the world.

In Detroit, we have raised hundreds of thousands of dollars from our community, and all that money, and clothing, drives for clothing and food and blankets, especially in the wintertime. That is also a critical time.

But our communities in northern Iraq, the Assyrians and the Chaldeans, they are basically prisoners in their own country. The other important issue is, and, Mr. Anderson, the Assyrians, the Chaldeans can't be gainfully employed in Kurdistan. Now, we have a problem with that.

Mr. SMITH. Yeah.

Mr. ORAM. You can't seek employment. Kurdistan, so far as I understand, is still a part of Iraq. Our people are basically depending on the diaspora communities for their survival. I have had conversations with folks from the United Nations, and they basically said when it came to the issue pertaining to the security of Nineveh and the communities in Syria and what have you, Qamishli and what have you, they basically said that they don't have the resources or they are not in a position to provide U.N. peacekeeping forces to protect those communities that are being threatened.

So, really, the United Nations really needs to step up to the plate.

Mr. SMITH. Yeah.

Mr. ORAM. And be a leader and providing a security apparatus. And, also, when—I would like to jump into the refugee issue. Yes, we have, as far as refugee admission to the United States, the Christians have really been—about we are 1 percent—less than 1 percent of admissions into this country. I am not here to have a debate about religion and about Islam and Christianity, but it seems 99 percent of the refugees that have been admitted into the United States are Muslim.

And when the United States basically was debating as to whether or not to declare this a genocide, their whole concern was, well, the Christians, they have options. They can pay jizya, a fee to basically stay alive. It took 1½ years for Secretary Kerry to make this declaration, and basically, all experts throughout the world came to the understanding and conclusion that this was actually a genocide, and I do commend the Secretary for finally making that declaration.

So, yeah, we need to really step up to the plate and provide financial assistance to these organizations and so the money can get to the communities.

Mr. SMITH. Yes.

Mr. HAMASAEED. Yeah, if I may just stress that the point I made in the written testimony as well, which the need today, whatever is seen by the international community, is far greater than what the system captures because the system does not see the amount, the volume of assistance that came from the local communities, from the Iraqis, whether in the Kurdistan region or the rest of the country. They have helped a lot in shouldering this and, actually, were the first responders in a way to the wave of crisis.

But I think, in addition to seeing the current need, we have to also look forward toward what would be the magnitude of the problem in a scenario of a protracted displacement a year from now, 2 years from now. A good number of those people will stay with us, and the kind of tensions that we see today in the housed communities, in the IDP camps, and a good number of people are outside the IDP camps, sometimes not registered in this system because of lack of documentations or the bureaucracy does not have the capacity to handle this magnitude.

Neither the Kurdistan Regional Government nor the Iraqi Government have handled something like this from a bureaucracy assistance standpoint. They don't have the capacity. Then there is the issue of resources. The communities have exhausted their resources that they have because of the economic downturn in Iraq. The drop in oil prices has strained the system. The country is fighting ISIL, so there are the military expenses. You have the destruction that comes from this fight. Ramadi: 80 percent destruction, other towns, the pictures are horrible. Sinjar, other minority places; the potential for return is a significant problem.

So the tensions will be something that we need to focus on. And it is important as we do this, there are issues that are directed at minorities from ISIL and other groups, but some of this is just a natural product of the chaos and the conflict where people do not have income and resources. They don't have jobs. There is a pressure on the governments of the region, in Iraq or elsewhere, to provide economic opportunities and give job permits. But the economy being down and people not having jobs is not just—you can go outside the camps, but there are no jobs.

There are many, many IDPs who have been interviewed, and they say: The economy outside is such that there is nobody to hire us because the economy is down. Oil prices are down. And the Kurdistan Regional Government and its tensions with Baghdad, they are late 3 months in the payment of their public servants. Their resources to help with the IDPs are far more limited.

So, therefore, the international community really takes this seriously from a humanitarian standpoint but also from a conflict prevention standpoint because the more displaced, the more—they either have to migrate, or there will be—they are vulnerable for other forms of radicalization as a response to the problem that they face.

Mr. SMITH. Ms. Kikoler.

Ms. KIKOLER. Thank you for raising that question, and maybe just to pick up on some of the things that Sarhang mentioned.

I think it is really important to underscore that the implications of the underfunding means that this crucial conversation about the day after—and in reality, we are talking about today. For areas that are already liberated around Sinjar, this is a question that people are grappling with today. Do people return? Can they return? Who is taking the leadership in pushing that conversation?

That discussion of the day after should be a central component of our counter-ISIL strategy conversations right now. All of us have highlighted a couple of components that usually fall outside, as Sarhang mentioned, of the traditional discussion of conflict prevention or counterterrorism. That is reconciliation, reconstruction, addressing political grievances, and the importance of accountability. Each of those require resources dedicated toward them, yet they are simply not a priority right now for many of the actors that we hope to take a leadership role in these particular issues.

Mr. SMITH. If you could just elaborate, not a priority for whom? The U.S. Government? The governments in the region?

Ms. Kikoler. I think it would be fair to say the international community, as a whole, has not been focused on this day after conversation, and I think there is an important role that Congress and others can play in raising that particular issue.

When we went to areas that had been newly liberated, to highlight what Sarhang mentioned, you see town after town and village after village that has been simply devastated: Homes that have been bombed; every gas station has been destroyed; water is down; electricity is beginning to be back in order. People are waiting to return home because they are waiting to see the schools in the Kurdish Regional Government close, waiting to see schools open now in newly liberated areas. Those are the types of urgent needs that need to be addressed and need to be part of that counter-ISIL strategy.

I think just to underscore a point that was made before too, those are not traditional kind of kinetic issues that need to be prioritized from an atrocity-prevention perspective, and it means that they are being viewed as second-order priorities whereas, really, they should be first-order priorities if we are hoping to prevent a recurrence of these crimes, and we need to do that with the recognition, as Sarhang said, that the capacity of the Government of Iraq and the capacity of the Kurdish Regional Government to address these issues is really quite diminished, and there are also concerns about the political will to address some of these particular concerns.

Mr. Crane. Thank you, Mr. Chairman.

As I am sitting here thinking of time and how long this conflict has gone on, I recall back in March 2011, I was asked by the Syrian National Congress at the time to meet with me and The Hague to talk about justice mechanisms that we could implement in the spring of 2011. It was a time of hope and excitement. It was the Free Syrian Army versus the Assad regime. It was not that completely simple, but that was pretty much it.

They were enthusiastic. They were listening, and I had been working with that group, along with the International Criminal Court, United Nations, and other countries in dealing with the transitional justice process. But dealing with my Syrian colleagues, I have noticed a sadness in their eyes, and they realize that this isn't going to go well, and I agree with them.

I particularly noticed, after the summer of 2013, when a certain line was drawn in the sand, saying: If you do this, then the international community will step in. It happened and nothing happened. And as we had been collating and putting in the crime base matrix events that have taken place that possibly could be war crimes, crimes against humanity, what have you, there was a pause in that summer of 2013 when the threat was made that if you do this, then we are going to step in. We actually saw, anecdotally, a decrease in atrocities. As soon as that line was drawn and was stepped over, then all hell broke loose, and we saw an increase in atrocities, which have gone off the chart since that time. Our crime base matrix at the Syrian Accountability Project is now over 7,000 pages of incidents that have taken place that could amount to international crimes.

So I just want to underscore, when we are talking about the urgency of time, we have now moved into an era where there is no practical solution to the Levant.

Mr. SMITH. I have some additional questions, which I will hold for a few moments, but I would like to yield to my friend and colleague, Ms. Bass, the ranking member.

Ms. BASS. Well, thank you, Mr. Chair. I appreciate you giving me the opportunity.

First of all, I would really like to thank all of the witnesses for not just your testimony but the work that you do. It has really been sobering.

I wanted to ask a couple of questions of you, Mr. Oram, about the Assyrian population in the U.S. You mentioned the Michigan area, and I was wondering, are there other places around the U.S. where there is a population?

And the other thing you mentioned was the population in Europe is experiencing some problems. It sounded like it was internal to the community, but I wonder if those same types of problems are being manifested in the United States.

Mr. ORAM. Thank you. Thank you very much, Ms. Bass.

We have, in the metro Detroit region, close to 200,000 Assyrians. We have been in the United States for decades. In addition to Detroit, there is a significant population of about 70,000 Assyrians in Chicago alone. And then we have communities in San Diego, Phoenix, and the Central Valley of California, the Modesto-Turlock area.

Ms. BASS. Uh-huh.

Mr. ORAM. So, yeah, we have a considerable population of our communities.

I will go to your Europe question on Europe, but as far as the problems here, no. When the the refugees immigrate to the United States, like specifically in Detroit, in particular, we have a community in Detroit that is so strong and well rooted, groundly rooted in the community, people in the community know who the Chaldeans and the Assyrians are. But, you will have your occasional individual or individuals that will basically categorize the Assyrians and the Chaldeans as being Arabs and Muslims and we are terrorists and what have you, but see, a lot of it is also about education. We go around to communities, and we educate policymakers all throughout the country and business leaders about who we are, what our identity is and our faith, and so that is extremely important.

But no. Our communities don't face violence here in the United States.

Ms. BASS. Uh-huh.

Mr. ORAM. This is the land of the free. This is the greatest country in the history of Earth.

And as far as Europe is concerned, yes, what is happening is a lot of the refugees are being grouped up, and it is not the governments that are really conducting this. It is basically the populace in some of these countries. Europe's borders are very porous.

Ms. BASS. Right.

Mr. ORAM. And so what is happening is, you know, we have our refugees that are in Sweden and all throughout Europe as Nuri

Kino, the investigative journalist and the founder of a Demand For Action, has spent 30 years documenting the issues of refugees and migration and what have you, and so there are communities in Europe where they face violence because of their faith.

Ms. BASS. Okay. Thank you. I appreciate that.

Mr. ORAM. Sure.

Ms. BASS. And then, Mr. Crane, I really admire what you have done in the past, and Mr. Smith has shared with me a few minutes ago about how you faced daily death threats during the time of Sierra Leone, and to come through that, you come through it with a certain amount of soberness.

I didn't particularly like to hear what you said, but I appreciate the reality. When you said that, one, you characterized it as Cold War ramifications, and I think you meant by that that this is nothing that is going to be solved quickly.

Mr. CRANE. Yes, ma'am.

Ms. BASS. But I appreciate you saying that because there is too much rhetoric out there about why don't we just do this and it fixes it, and I think you painted a far more realistic picture, and I appreciate that, even though it was difficult to hear.

So I wanted to know if you would elaborate a little more about some of the solutions that you talked about. You talked about a Marshall Plan. I was wondering what your vision would be as to who would come together to do that.

You talked about holding ISIS accountable, and you mentioned a hybrid court, and I wanted to understand what exactly that meant, how that would be.

What you went through in Sierra Leone, trying to imagine holding ISIS accountable like that when the leadership is so diffuse. How would you hold ISIS accountable? What are some of your thoughts about that?

Why don't we start there?

Mr. CRANE. Thank you, Ms. Bass.

I appreciate your comments, and I think your questions are very, very important. What I really wanted to underscore in my comments this afternoon is that this truly is a decades-long effort. In this age, where we try to solve problems within 24 hours, it just can't be done.

After World War II and facing the Cold War and the challenge of the Soviet Union, the world got together and created the political will to face down the Iron Curtain and what was behind it. We created NATO. We moved into Korea. We are still in Korea.

Ms. BASS. Uh-huh, right.

Mr. CRANE. 1950. NATO is a successful example of a commitment by the world to stop tyranny. So there is historical precedent if there is the political will to come in and begin a process, begin a process where we have the international community, administered probably by the region where we have the International Monetary Fund, the World Bank, others where we have funds where instead of spending billions dollars a week bombing what we perceive to be a threat and creating job programs.

I mean, what a wonderful thing it is to see almost like a Civilian Conservation Corps out there creating roads and building and reconstructing the damage that has been done. Again, I know it is not that simple, but at least if we change and shift our emphasis on construction as opposed to destruction, I think that we have a better chance in succeeding. So that was what I meant by the Marshall Plan.

Ms. BASS. Let me interrupt you for just a minute about that. Okay.

Mr. CRANE. Yes, ma'am.

Ms. BASS. One, I would love to see that actually here with our infrastructure, our failing infrastructure, and need for jobs. But this is what confuses me, and that is, who would the actors be?

Because post-World War II—I mean, and most of what you described in terms of International Monetary Fund, World Bank, et cetera, are European based, you know what I mean, and how—what parts of the region come together considering, you know, whether they are actively involved or not, how would you have the European-based powers then go in and say here is a Marshall Plan for what is predominantly the Arab world?

Mr. CRANE. Well, again, an excellent question and probably an unanswerable question as far as political will. We just have to step back and stop using kinetic energy to solve the problems in the Middle East. It is not working, and yet we take all of those billions and, in some cases, now probably trillions——

Ms. BASS. Trillions, right.

Mr. CRANE [continuing]. Of dollars, and we could have shifted that in a way that would have revitalized an area. Not making it a religious base, not making it Sunni versus Shia or Christian versus Muslim, an ability for the region, backed by Arab states as well, with some leadership by the European Union, what have you, to do this.

It is not going to be easy.

Ms. BASS. Uh-huh.

Mr. CRANE. But I am just trying to get a conversation going and asking the question, can we do better than just kinetic energy, bombing our way out of a solution?

Ms. BASS. I appreciate that.

Mr. CRANE. So, again, forgive me for not being able to give you specific answers because——

Ms. BASS. That is okay.

Mr. CRANE [continuing]. I don't, but I think that changing our perspective will certainly be important.

Now, you also bring up a—the hybrid court idea. At the end of the day, this is all about the victims, right. We are very arrogant about how we approach international justice. We don't have all the solutions. There are certainly other justice methodologies. I always used to ask the question, is the justice we seek the justice they want? I think that is really an important question because we tend to think that the European model of international justice or the common law model is the model, but some of these justice mechanisms in other parts of the world have been around for thousands of years and have worked.

So we have to be very, very humble to realize what do the victims in Syria and in the Levant and in northern Iraq, what is justice to them? And once we begin to consider that, there are many, many possibilities, and it may not be an international system. So a hybrid court or a domestic court or internationalized domestic court may be something that may be important. Even going back and looking at tribal and cultural type of methods of justice may be a start or a beginning.

How would you hold members of ISIS accountable? Well, of course, that is a challenge. I think that once we were able to do that—that is part and parcel to this overall A plus B plus C plus D step forward, is begin to try to contain ISIS. A good example is ISIS is like a cancer that is not going to cause a fatal result, but it is there, and so your doctor is going to have to say: We are going to have to manage this.

Ms. BASS. Uh-huh.

Mr. CRANE. And so we should manage ISIS like such, try to cut out areas that they try to grow in other parts of the world, Libya, for example, and other parts. Deal with those smaller problems, but try to contain ISIS, and then begin to develop many things, to include a justice mechanism where it can be seen that the international community, the region itself is actually doing something.

It doesn't have to be elaborate. It can be just a simple step of creating a truth commission where we have the trust being garnered. Again, if you build it, they will come. I have been told, well, you can't have a truth commission for these various reasons, what have you. Well, we have got to do something. We have got to be seen at doing something in the transitional justice area other than talking about various ways that we can go about that.

That is just a simple example. But this is all part and parcel to a larger achievable results: Contain ISIS and begin to pick out areas where we can succeed so we can bring back that hope, which robs ISIS of its ability to recruit, and that cancer begins to shrink.

Now, again, there are many, many levels of problems here that could throw this off the rails. But we just have to look at this a little bit more simply and a little bit more objectively and step back and go what really is working and what really isn't working, and I will guarantee you, it is not using kinetic energy.

Ms. BASS. Thank you. Thank you very much.

Mr. CRANE. Yes, ma'am.

Ms. BASS. I yield back.

Mr. HAMASAEED. Just quickly on the question of justice, this is something that the U.S. Institute of Peace is dealing within areas that have been liberated, because we have the experience that we are looking at, like, what does that look like? And that—this is closer to Salahuddin and not directly minority areas. But the issue of justice where you have tribes, they have their local mechanisms that usually they go for revenge and there is exacting blood money, and these have complicated the situation.

In the case of Tikrit, after what is known as Camp Speicher where ISIL killed 1,700 soldiers and cadets, we managed to tap into those local traditions through facilitated dialogue—using facilitators USIP trained over the years—there is a level of venting that needs to take place among those actors. That happened. And then they engaged on the substance. They realized that going into this cycle of violence will change the nature of the problem, and it will make things more complex.

So there are ways that you can deal with this and tap into those local solutions and prevent violence. There was a question of justice. So, for those who have been killed, for those who have been displaced, what does justice look like? And there is no universal answer. It really varies depending on what the different communities accept. In Tikrit, they decided they will work with the judicial system of the government. The tribe said: We will work with the system, and we will bring perpetrators to justice, and we will work with you.

In a town few miles away, in Yathrib, Salahuddin, the local population, to date, are not allowing people to return because they do not necessarily accept that other local solution. And the government doesn't have the capacity to deal with the justice of ISIS because, as you alluded to, these are fragmented members. It is not an entity that you can go to one place and capture them.

And unless the local population cooperates with this process to help you identify who did this and what, then it will be very difficult to bring perpetrators to justice. And I have to warn about after 2003, de-Ba'athification was getting rid of the members of Ba'ath party was a big problem, contributed in the way it was dealt with to giving the—add to the problem of today. Actually, the day after of this problem, liberated areas, I think this is our problem: Going after those labeled as collaborating with ISIS and then what will be the ramification for the political process? For the stabilization? For the next cycle of the problem?

So putting energy and resources and building it bottom up, tapping into both what the system can do, but also really getting the community to work with this issue because they have seen it in the most painful way now. They have been displaced. They have seen their people killed. I think there could be an opening to tap into that and build upon that. But if we just leave it like this, I think it will fester, and this will become the underestimated problem that we face.

Many people underestimated that the vacuum in Iraq could give us ISIS in its current form. And then there was underestimation of the damage that ISIS could do and the response needed. I think the post-ISIS situation also is probably underestimated right now and could use more attention. Thank you.

Ms. KIKOLER. Thank you very much.

One of the purposes of our recent trip was also to look at issues relating to accountability and justice, hence our recommendation around the need to prioritize transitional justice. And just very briefly, I think there are five points that I would make.

The first is there is a need for there to be an independent international investigation into what happened to ensure that there can be the collection of evidence and the preservation of evidence and their analysis in accordance with international standards, to help establish truth, to help families identify what happened to their loved ones, and to push for future prosecutions and accountability.

The second is that there needs to be an investment in supporting the capacity building and rule of law efforts of the Government of Iraq and the Kurdish Regional Government. That is needed immediately, but it will have long-term benefits to ensure that the rule of law actually means something and that minority communities feel that should their rights be violated in the future, they can resort to courts and not have to take up other means to protect themselves.

The third is both the Government of Iraq and the Kurdish Regional Government currently lack legislation that allows them to prosecute genocide. There is an effort under way to create such legislation. The political will to do so is mixed. There is an important role that the international community can play in pushing for the enactment of that legislation so that we could possibly see cases brought at the national level.

The fourth, as I mentioned earlier, is the importance and priority that should be placed on local cases, trying people for murder, for these kind of property seizures, for what happened in their own communities, and there is an important issue that arises on that. It requires the detaining of people and the investigation for future prosecutions.

Now, many Islamic State fighters tend to blow themselves up or killed on the battlefield. It is unclear for those who are being detained by different forces what is happening to them. We need to do a better job of trying to arrest people, ensure that there can be future prosecutions with them. That is going to be very pertinent when we see a liberation of Mosul. And it is going to raise a lot of challenging human rights questions about the vetting of people as they flee Mosul in ensuring that not all Sunni Arabs are stopped and detained and assumed that they are Islamic State supporters but that those few that have actually committed crimes are actually held responsible.

And then, finally, to underscore the point that Sarhang made about the critical need to support local civil society that is undertaking these efforts to do documentation but also to do the conflict management and mediation and reconciliation work that will be so critical to ensuring that we don't see a further recurrence of atrocities.

Mr. SMITH. Thank you, Ms. Bass.

And thank you.

Just some final questions.

Mr. Anderson, you pointed out in your testimony that American policy should recognize the important differences in the situation of those fleeing violence and those targeted for genocide, and we should prioritize the latter, and I would add with emphasis, especially since the administration has made the designation of genocide against Christians and other minority faiths.

Consider this analogy, you point out, after World War II, there were approximately 50 million refugees. Only a small fraction were Jews, yet the world understood that Jews who have survived genocide faced a qualitatively different situation and deserved heightened consideration.

I believe strongly—and if you want to elaborate on that—that you could put exclamation points on that for the Christians, the Yazidis. Today, when they can't even get into an UNHCR or IDP camp or a refugee camp, are unwanted, at risk, and as you pointed out, a news report showed or indicated that of the 499 Syrian refugees admitted to the United States in May, not one, I repeat and say again, not one was listed as being Christian or as explicitly coming from any of the groups targeted for genocide.

To me, that has got to change. I mean, that is unconscionable. It is not like we haven't been raising this for, in my case, 3 years. In the cases of so many others, 3 years, and we have had hearing after hearing. You talk about protecting, and Ms. Kikoler, your point about civilian protection as being a core, I think, is very well placed. It has not been, and maybe you might want to elaborate on, do you sense that it is becoming a core protection, especially in light of the genocide statement?

And let me also ask about the idea of stabilization, and again, there is so much overlap, great minds think alike, and you five have provided expert testimony, and there are a number of areas where there is an overlap of concern and recommendation. I chair the Commission on Security and Cooperation in Europe and have been very involved for years on Bosnia, was actually in Vukovar right before it fell, before Serbia conquered it 3 or 4 weeks before it fell, and worked very hard with the Yugoslav court to hold people who committed those atrocities to account.

Well, the whole idea of stabilization, one of our members of the full committee, Scott Perry, was part of the stabilization force and can tell you, as was mentioned earlier by Professor Crane, we are still in Korea. The stabilization force, it took years, and I remember being in burnt-out homes throughout Bosnia. I was actually in Srebrenica, where the genocide against Muslims occurred, which was horrific. I was there for one of the re-interment ceremonies.

My point being, we do have to plan for that post-conflict when there is a liberated area? I am concerned we are not doing the kind of aggressive planning that is necessary. Because we had forces on the ground in Tuzla and elsewhere, we did a lot of that. It still wasn't perfect.

But get this, as of yesterday, and I had a hearing on Bosnia, there are still approximately 800 people who committed horrific crimes in Bosnia, mostly against Muslims, who the criminal court for the former Yugoslavia devolved to the local courts, and they— not one—not one—have been taken up.

So the importance of the courts can't be overstated as a means of meting out justice and giving the survivors at least some peace that their next door neighbor or the guy that is one block away wasn't someone who was putting bullets in the heads of family members or committing acts of torture.

I do meet frequently with these folks in Bosnia, and if we don't have lessons learned from all of that, shame on us. So all the more reason why a court needs to be set up.

And I really, really appreciate again, Professor, your point about the cornerstone of a possible beginning of the solution is to get Arab resolve in cooperation. The idea of having Arab states prosecuting Arabs for crimes against Arab peoples in violation of Arab laws, the idea that at least you have ownership, and I think that is a very, very important point for all. We want to lend and assist.

And, again, on capacity, as was mentioned by some of our witnesses, you, in Sierra Leone, left not only well-trained prosecutors and people who understood rule of law and how to garner evidence and present it in court, you left buildings where people could work and do the important work of justice. And I think all the more reason why we need to push that.

But if you could speak to these questions that I am raising—all of you or some of you, however you would like—I would appreciate it.

Maybe start with you, Mr. Anderson, on this. We have got the designation. Why aren't Christians being focused upon? There is no religious test here. I think the President erred when he said we don't have religious tests. When Jackson-Vanik passed and the Soviet Union and Jews were escaping the horrific psychiatric prisons of the Soviet Union, and I actually went to Perm Camp 35, where a number of political and religious prisoners were—and it was terrible—but we saved hundreds of thousands of Jews through limiting MFN to the Soviet Union based on focusing on Jewish people who were being so persecuted by the Soviet Union.

We are talking about minority faiths here. We need to redouble our efforts, as you pointed out on the Tom Cotton bill, and thank you for that. Well, maybe you want to elaborate, if you would.

Mr. ANDERSON. Thank you for the question, Mr. Chairman, and especially for your leadership for so many years on this.

It goes without saying: Every human life has dignity, has sanctity. We should do whatever we can to support each individual who is in these tragic situations, and of course, the help that we are doing, as I mentioned, helping Yazidis, helping Muslims, there is not a distinction of helping the individuals. But I think we have to realize a basic reality here, that there are minority, indigenous communities that have been in these lands for thousands of years, and they are going to be extinguished. And that is a different qualitative reality. And so what the world has to ask itself is, are we going to allow that to happen? Are we going to allow it to happen?

And, therefore, if the decision is, no, we are not going to allow this, then we have to make special efforts. We have to give special attention to preserve these communities. It is just as simple as that. Nobody wants to apply religious tests, but the fact is these people, these communities, this heritage will be gone unless we do something extra to save it.

Mr. SMITH. Answer to any of those questions?

Mr. ORAM. Thank you very much, Mr. Chairman. Again, I commend you for your leadership in spending so many years in this respective body fighting for religious freedoms throughout the world.

Mr. Anderson is correct. The Assyrian and the Chaldean communities of Iraq and Syria do face extinction, but another problem that I would like to kind of touch on is the central government in Baghdad. After the war, the Coalition Provisional Authority dialogued with the Iraqis in basically implementing Article 125, the redrafting of the Iraqi Constitution with Article 125 which basically talked about the protection of Iraq's Christian minorities. Article 125 is a moot point right now. The Iraqi Government has failed in upholding its constitutional duties. When the Islamic State came barreling through many towns and villages of the Nineveh plains, the Iraqi Army, 50,000-60,000 and some odd to about 10,000 or 9,000 thugs, basically, surrendered and basically relinquished their weapons, arms, clothing, and uniforms and fled. That is basically negligence on the Iraqi Government's part. We can basically sit here and point fingers about they did this and play the blame game, but let's move forward. I urge that this Congress basically urge the Iraqi Government to step up to the plate and help these communities, everything from financial assistance to each individual that has been impacted because, again, the Iraqi Government has a moral and fundamental responsibility to protect its citizens, and they failed. Thank you.

Mr. SMITH. Thank you. If I could, and Professor Crane, if you could, in addition to those questions, in your statement, you talk about the Syracuse Syrian Accountability Project, which you have founded: Over the past 5-plus years, we have built a trial package that a domestic, regional, or international prosecutor can consider in developing a case against all parties committing atrocity in the Levant. This package includes a conflict map, a crime base matrix, and other associated documents to include sample indictments. And you pointed out how you used that very same technique in successfully prosecuting Charles Taylor and other henchmen.

Can you elaborate on that because that is absolutely vital, I think, to the future of successful prosecution? It is not like it all has to be reinvented. Don't reinvent the wheel. You have ready-made tools here.

Mr. CRANE. I think it is very important that we do understand that we have made great strides in the past 20 years in international criminal law. Most of this was theory when I was in law school or not even taught because it didn't even exist. What we do now, we have this capacity, the rules of evidence, the practical experience, and the jurisprudence to prosecute and hold accountable any individual who commits atrocities, international crimes. Again, the bright red thread of all of this is politics, and that is always, always a challenge related to dealing with these types of issues. But at the end of the day, because we have this practical experience now of taking down and holding accountable a head of state, his henchmen, for what they have done to a region, we need to continue to work together to use those techniques so that someday, whether it be tomorrow, next year, or 10 years, we will have that ability then to hold accountable those who have destroyed this area of the world.

So we do have a conflict map. We have literally developed a criminal history of the Syrian conflict and in the Levant since March 2011. We continue to monitor that and write that chapter. We also have that crime base matrix, which lists by date, time, location, perpetrator, as well as the specific violation of the Rome Statute, international humanitarian laws, such as the Geneva Conventions, and we have translated the Syrian criminal code, which is a good criminal code, one that could be used for the basis for domestic prosecutions, into English. And so we have also identified by paragraph and line the violations of Syrian law as well. That particular aspect of the Syrian Accountability Project now numbers over 7,000 pages. In fact, there is so much of it that we have put it into a memory stick because I can't transport that around. In fact, the chairman knows; I gave him a copy of that last week. Now we share this. This is not all about the Syrian Accountability Project at Syracuse University College of Law. This is about justice for the people of Syria. So we share all of this data, and have since

March 2011, with our colleagues in the United Nations, various key countries, such as the United States, our friends in the war crimes office there, along with the international criminal accord. I personally give this data to the chief prosecutor, Fatou Bensouda, as well. So we are sharing. We are working with other important accountability organizations to work together to make sure that, again, at the end of the day, it is about the victims and justice for the victims.

But one caution here. You know, 10, 12 years ago, when I was investigating west Africa, we went out and did it the old way, cops going out, gathering evidence, taking statements and what have you. Now, with this social media age, we are inundated by a tsunami of information. It is too much. The challenge now is not finding the evidence. The challenge is now finding the evidence in a haystack. Ninety-nine-point-nine percent of the data coming out of Syria in whatever capacity being held by whatever organization is not evidence. We cannot use it in a court of law. I think that is really important for us to understand. It is a great historical body of information. It is important in many other ways, but it can't be used in court. I think we tend to forget that, that we have all this information, but it is just information. It is not evidence. And so I think we have to be very, very careful when we say we have cases against all these individuals. The answer is we may have cases against these individuals, and we have to be very, very careful. But, again, that is up to a prosecutor, a local, regional, or international prosecutor, to take this and hopefully take our trial package and use it in whatever way he or she can use it in order to seek justice for the people of the Levant region.

Mr. SMITH. Before we conclude, anything else that any witness would like to—yes, Ms. Kikoler.

Ms. KIKOLER. Just in light of the question that you asked about the integration of civilian protection, I think it is really important to underscore that defeating ISIS but failing to prevent atrocities and provide adequate security to all Iraqis will likely fuel future grievances, a proliferation of armed groups, and continued conflict. In our original report, we highlighted that the current counterterrorism and counterinsurgency paradigms don't prioritize an assessment of or compel a response to, in a systematic way, the unique threats and risks of mass atrocities that local populations and individuals may face, so, as a result, going forward, we do feel that it is important to prioritize the mapping of the motivations, organizations, and capabilities of perpetrators and the vulnerabilities of at-risk communities.

Finding proactive ways to identify where these communities are, our report focused on Iraq—there are communities in Syria that remain at risk: Mapping their location, tracking the movement and mobilization of potential perpetrators, and identifying other actors that enable or inhibit the perpetration of mass atrocity crimes. This includes intelligence gathering and analysis that plays a critical role in developing the strategies that will be used to provide protection for communities and prevent future atrocities going forward.

Mr. SMITH. Could I ask you, on that parallel, if you would, would a safe haven, is that more of a surface appeal but strewn with a number of challenges that may make it unachievable, or is it something that ought to be, in your opinion, promoted?

Ms. KIKOLER. I think, from our perspective, there are a host of questions that need to be asked about how to provide protection, and we don't necessarily go into military strategies at the Museum ourselves. I think the questions that can be asked about areas like safe havens and other options are, what are the specific threats facing civilian populations? What are the resources that are needed to provide protection? What are the various options that are available to ensure that, over a sustained period of time, communities will be protected and a host of other scenarios?

In the case of northern Iraq, one of the things that we have highlighted is the need to focus on addressing the deep distrust that communities feel toward others and recognizing that the areas that we are talking about are not ethnically or religiously homogenous. Communities live alongside each other, and any discussion about local administration, physical protection, has to take into account those realities in that particular area, but I think others would probably be more well-versed.

Mr. SMITH. Yes.

Mr. HAMASAEED. Yes. So I think that it is important to look at the different scenarios that we talked about, the protracted stay but also the scenario of return. The whole system is struggling with providing food and assistance, so that is a level of need we are talking about, and the scenario of return, there is a physical protection of those people, and then ideas, such as safe havens and all of that, there are practicality elements that need to be taken into consideration.

Okay. What objective will that serve? So, in the past, a safe haven, again, is a system like Saddam Hussein could have—a systemic protection would have been helpful, but right now, the threat is far more retail in the sense of you have a terror organization that knows no boundaries. And then you have the fear of revenge that is actually at the individual and tribal and family level sometimes. So a safe haven or the concept of protection and physical protection, that changes how you deliver that. This is where the better relationship with the neighboring communities and working on that becomes necessary. And I think one of the things that could be helpful for the Iraqi minorities—as important as they make this case, as they present solutions—some of the solutions will create other problems, will create other conflicts and other competition. It is important that at this moment of frustration and this moment of anger—and it is a lot, and they have every right to be angry and frustrated and disappointed. But getting back to what Mr. Crane said about achievable programs and achievable objectives, it is important to look at a framework solution for Iraq. Without fixing that, the minorities will always be caught in between those.

I would like to stress that the military approach is probably important for certain problems, but it will not solve the long term. And preserving those communities, you may be physically safe if you relocate to the Kurdistan region or you relocate to outside, but preserving the community, as a community—and for Sabean-Mandeans, their numbers have dropped over the years to about a couple of thousand worldwide. This is how you lose a community.

The Christians have seen their numbers drop from about 1.5 million in 2003 now to about less than a third of that in Iraq. Preserving the sense of community will require for the minorities to be striking those relationships with those Iraqi communities for the long term. But also the civil society and the external assistance could go also into preserving those communities in terms of education, in terms of programs that will provide services to those areas. And this is what the Alliance of Iraqi Minorities has done very successfully: Working with the Iraqi Government and with the Kurdistan Regional Government. Those efforts could help the minorities help themselves, be the voice of the community, and engage the international actors.

Mr. SMITH. Thank you.

Mr. Oram.

Mr. ORAM. Thank you, Mr. Chairman, for touching on the safe haven question. You know, right now, a good number of our people do not want to return back to their villages and towns in the Nineveh plains because they have lost the confidence and the trust of not only their government, but remember, a lot of their Sunni neighbors in the villages essentially marked them for death. They basically went ahead and etched on the big "N" for Nazarene, identifying them as Christian families, but the only way for an effective safe haven mechanism is obviously laying a foundation for the successful liberation of Mosul, which is basically the gateway of Iraq's Christian region, and also to ensure that the Assyrian communities of northern Iraq enjoy their own self-autonomous identity, their own affairs, as well as a security apparatus through the support of our Government. That is the only way that they can have their confidence and their hopes restored, by having a security mechanism in place, their own autonomy, dictating their own policies and what have you. This is extremely important for a long-term effort, for fulfilling a safe haven for our communities in northern Iraq.

And that is why it is important now to address this and this is going to be a long process, and so I think, right now, we really need to identify the current situation at hand with respect to the IDPs, the violence and the harassment, the lack of aid that they are receiving, as well as reforming our immigration or Refugee Act of 1980, designating new visas, the P-2 and the P-3 visas, for many of these Christian families to come to the United States. And a lot of them have relatives and friends and families in the United States. They can come back here and join them. This is important, but I think it should be a part of our long-term foreign policy strategy to preserve Christianity in the Middle East. We are the oldest in civilization. We are the indigenous peoples, and it is vital to America's national security to make sure that this is reached.

Thank you very much, Mr. Chairman.

Mr. SMITH. I want to thank each and every one of you for your time, your leadership, for taking the time to present very, very incisive testimonies to the committee, and we will share this with a large number of people, so thank you, and I look forward to working with you going forward.

The hearing is adjourned.

[Whereupon, at 2:17 p.m., the subcommittee was adjourned.]

A P P E N D I X

68

SUBCOMMITTEE HEARING NOTICE
COMMITTEE ON FOREIGN AFFAIRS
U.S. HOUSE OF REPRESENTATIVES
WASHINGTON, DC 20515-6128

Subcommittee on Africa, Global Health, Global Human Rights, and International Organizations
Christopher H. Smith (R-NJ), Chairman

May 26, 2016

TO: MEMBERS OF THE COMMITTEE ON FOREIGN AFFAIRS

You are respectfully requested to attend an OPEN hearing of the Committee on Foreign Affairs, to be held by the Subcommittee on Africa, Global Health, Global Human Rights, and International Organizations in Room 2172 of the Rayburn House Office Building (and available live on the Committee website at http://www.ForeignAffairs.house.gov):

DATE: Thursday, May 26, 2016

TIME: 12:00 p.m.

SUBJECT: The ISIS Genocide Declaration: What Next?

WITNESSES: Mr. Carl A. Anderson
Supreme Knight
Knights of Columbus

Mr. Sarhang Hamasaeed
Senior Program Officer
Middle East and Africa Programs
U.S. Institute of Peace

Mr. Johnny Oram
Executive Director
Chaldean Assyrian Business Alliance

Mr. David M. Crane
Professor of Practice
Syracuse University College of Law
(Former Chief Prosecutor, United Nations Special Court for Sierra Leone)

Ms. Naomi Kikoler
Deputy Director
Simon-Skjodt Center for the Prevention of Genocide
United States Holocaust Memorial Museum

By Direction of the Chairman

COMMITTEE ON FOREIGN AFFAIRS

MINUTES OF SUBCOMMITTEE ON _Africa, Global Health, Global Human Rights, and International Organizations_ HEARING

Day _Thursday_ Date _May 26, 2016_ Room _2172 Rayburn HOB_

Starting Time _12:03 p.m._ Ending Time _2:17 p.m._

Recesses | _0_ | (___ to ___)(___ to ___)(___ to ___)(___ to ___)(___ to ___)(___ to ___)

Presiding Member(s)

Rep. Chris Smith

Check all of the following that apply:

Open Session ☑   Electronically Recorded (taped) ☑
Executive (closed) Session ☐   Stenographic Record ☑
Televised ☑

TITLE OF HEARING:

The ISIS Genocide Declaration: What Next?

SUBCOMMITTEE MEMBERS PRESENT:

Rep. Karen Bass

NON-SUBCOMMITTEE MEMBERS PRESENT: _(Mark with an * if they are not members of full committee.)_

Rep. Dana Rohrabacher

HEARING WITNESSES: Same as meeting notice attached? Yes ☑ No ☐
(If "no", please list below and include title, agency, department, or organization.)

STATEMENTS FOR THE RECORD: _(List any statements submitted for the record.)_

U.S. Holocaust Memorial Museum Report - Our Generation is Gone - The Islamic State's Targeting of Iraqi Minorities in Ninewa, submitted by Ms. Naomi Kikoler
Ninevah Plains Paper by Mr. Gregory Kruczek, submitted by Rep. Chris Smith
Documenting Genocide White Paper, submitted by Rep. Chris Smith

TIME SCHEDULED TO RECONVENE _____
or
TIME ADJOURNED _2:17 p.m._

Subcommittee Staff Associate

Material submitted for the record by Ms. Naomi Kikoler, deputy director, Simon-Skjodt Center for the Prevention of Genocide, United States Holocaust Memorial Museum

BEARING WITNESS TRIP REPORT

"OUR GENERATION IS GONE" The Islamic State's Targeting of Iraqi Minorities in Ninewa

UNITED STATES HOLOCAUST MEMORIAL MUSEUM

SIMON-SKJODT CENTER FOR THE PREVENTION OF GENOCIDE

A Yezidi man who lives in a displaced persons camp.

SUMMARY OF KEY FINDINGS

THE COMMISSION OF CRIMES

- The self-proclaimed Islamic State (IS) perpetrated crimes against humanity, ethnic cleansing, and war crimes against Christian, Yezidi, Turkmen, Shabak, Sabaean-Mandaean, and Kaka'i people in Ninewa province between June and August 2014.

- We believe IS has been and is perpetrating genocide against the Yezidi people.

- IS's stated intent and patterns of violence against Shia Shabak and Shia Turkmen also raise concerns about the commission and risk of genocide against these groups and requires further investigation.

- Men, women, and children who were kidnapped and are still being held by IS continue to be the victims of atrocity crimes. Their release must be a priority.

- IS perpetrated these crimes in accordance with its extremist religious ideology—targeting particular groups on the basis of their identity.

- IS also perpetrated mass atrocities as part of a deliberate military, economic, and political strategy. This intent was matched by the group's ability to carry out these crimes.

- Under IS's ideology, adherents of religions considered infidel or apostate—including Yezidis—are to be converted or killed and members of other religions—such as Christians—are to be subjected to expulsion, extortion, or forced conversion.

- The Iraqi government bears the primary responsibility to protect its population from mass atrocities and has failed to do so.

RESPONSE

- Since 2003, violence and instability in Iraq has put minorities at risk of atrocities. The risk factors, where known, include:
  - A pattern of mass atrocities perpetrated against Iraqi minorities by Sunni and Shia extremists since 2003;
  - A strong Sunni extremist presence as well as confusion over the provision of protection for minorities by Iraqi and Kurdish regional authorities in Ninewa;
  - A lack of effective strategies for protection within minority communities, including through self-defense or by external actors. Flight was their only option.

- Chronic instability, sectarianism, and rampant impunity allowed for the persecution of minorities and for extremism to fester, thereby creating conditions under which future atrocity crimes could be perpetrated.

- The early warning signs of potential atrocities against minority populations went largely unnoticed, or were misdiagnosed, meaning that preventive strategies that could have mitigated the risk to these populations were not developed.

THE WAY FORWARD

- Any response to IS and affiliated groups should incorporate at its core an atrocity prevention framework that includes risk assessments; the provision of genuine physical protection to vulnerable populations; accountability for crimes perpetrated by IS and Iraqi and Kurdish security forces, as well as state-aligned militias; and strategies intended to address the root causes and drivers of conflict and atrocities in Iraq.

- Going forward, the way the war against IS is fought will influence whether there will be a recurrence of atrocities—winning the war but failing to prevent atrocities and provide adequate security to **ALL** Iraqis will likely fuel future grievances, a proliferation of armed actors, and continued conflict.

- Countering IS necessitates an ongoing assessment of its motivations, organization, and capabilities for committing atrocity crimes, and of the vulnerabilities of at-risk communities.

- When done effectively, both counterterrorism and atrocity prevention advance core US national security interests. These goals should be seen as mutually reinforcing rather than as an additional burden or strain on limited resources.

- Building trust and fostering accountability between communities, especially between Sunni Arab and minority populations, must accompany any counter-IS strategy.

- Unable to return home until their land is liberated, internally displaced persons (IDPs) face prolonged displacement. Under these conditions, they will remain in dire need of humanitarian assistance and physical protection.

- IDPs' ethnic and religious identities must be preserved—including by upholding their freedom of religion, expression, and language.

MATERIAL SUBMITTED FOR THE RECORD BY THE HONORABLE CHRISTOPHER H. SMITH, A REPRESENTATIVE IN CONGRESS FROM THE STATE OF NEW JERSEY, AND CHAIRMAN, SUBCOMMITTEE ON AFRICA, GLOBAL HEALTH, GLOBAL HUMAN RIGHTS, AND INTERNATIONAL ORGANIZATIONS

To be Submitted For the Record on May 26, 2016
-to-
The House Foreign Affairs Subcommittee on Africa, Global Health, Global Human Rights, and International Organizations meeting
"The ISIS Genocide Declaration: What's Next?"

The Nineveh Plains: Why Calls for a Minority Safe-Haven are Shortsighted, Unrealistic, and Ultimately Bad for Iraq and its Minorities

Author: Gregory J. Kruczek, Ph.D. Candidate, Virginia Tech University, Government and International Affairs

Last week Rep. Jeff Fortenberry (R-NE) attempted to introduce amendments to H.R. 4909, which appropriates funds for the Department of Defense. The amendments included: "Securing safe areas, including the Nineveh Plains, for purposes of resettling and reintegrating ethnic and religious minorities, including victims of genocide, into their homelands....." The call for a safe area or safe-haven is noble. Rep. Fortenberry's efforts help spread awareness of a situation veering toward genocide.

However, a safe-haven stands little chance of coming to fruition due to the massive coordination and governance effort(s) it would take from a multitude of different and competing actors. It fails to take into account the altered inter-group dynamic in Nineveh between Muslims and non-Muslims, as well as the scale of reconciliation efforts needed to heal those cleavages. It ignores the territory's strategic importance to Baghdad and Erbil, especially as it relates to the post-ISIL invasion facts on the ground. Finally, it fails to provide a long-term security and political solution for the minorities of Nineveh, specifically their integration into a federal Iraq as part of the Nineveh Plains Governorate.

The Nineveh Plains, Religious Minorities, and ISIL

The Nineveh Plains stretch north and east from Mosul, encompassing the districts of Tel Kef, Shekhan, and Hamdaniya. A section of the Nineveh Plains is considered part of the Disputed Territories of Iraq. The forces of the Islamic State in Iraq and the Levant (ISIL) stormed into Nineveh in June 2014. Iraqi security forces disintegrated. Mosul, Iraq's second largest city, along with a large portion the surrounding region, fell under ISIL's control. ISIL then launched a violent campaign against its enemies, particularly the religious minorities like Assyrians, Yezidis, Turkomen, and Shabaks that have historically called the Nineveh Plains home. Assistant Secretary for the Bureau of Democracy, Human Rights, and Labor Tom Malinowski testified to Congress the following September about reports of:

> "(E)xtrajudicial and mass killings, beheadings, abductions, forced conversions, torture, rape and sexual assault, using women and

children as human shields, and people being burned or buried alive..."

ISIL's Iraqi gains are slowly being reversed. But the most important battle, the battle for Mosul and the rest of the Nineveh Plains, has been pending for almost two years.

The Coordination and Governance Problem

The primary shortcomings of a plan to secure a minority safe-haven in the Nineveh Plains are coordination and governance. The U.S., the Iraqi Government, the KRG, Shia and other local militias, Sunni tribesman, and Iran each retain a strong desire to defeat ISIL. Yet each actor also has its own agenda for Iraq. Political paralysis in Baghdad and ongoing corruption in Erbil remain a significant hindrance.

Two years removed from the Iraqi Army's retreat from Mosul, effective military coordination between Iraq's military forces, the popular mobilization forces, Kurdish Peshmerga, and the country's external patrons to retake ISIL occupied sections of Iraq is, to say the least, wanting. Washington and Tehran have invested too much in Iraq to see it go the other's way. The Kurds are eyeing independence and (re)claiming portions of The Disputed Territories of Iraq. The Al-Abadi regime in Baghdad is rightfully preoccupied with remaining in power, holding the country together, and instituting much needed political reforms. In short, no actor has demonstrated the will or ability to act unilaterally to impose a minority safe-haven. It is therefore unlikely these same actors with their conflicting agendas will work together to plan, implement, and administer and secure such an area.

There is also the post-ISIL governance issue. Prior to ISIL, much of Iraq's Sunni population in and outside of Mosul felt neglected by Baghdad. Prioritizing the establishment of a safe-haven over Iraq's second largest city would send the residents of Mosul and Iraq at large a message that Baghdad was indeed uninterested in good governance. In addition, the Iraqi population's memories of sectarian violence during the U.S. occupation are still fresh. Some of Iraq's Arab-Muslim population may thus see the creation of a minority safe-haven, which Christians would constitute a sizeable portion of, as colonialism at work *(It is thought that Christians made up close to 40% of the population of the Nineveh Plains pre-ISIL invasion)*. Iraq does not need any additional ethnic particularism, real or imagined.

The (Displaced) Residents of Nineveh

A secure and stable post-ISIL northern Iraq will require a massive inter-group reconciliation effort. Many displaced persons were betrayed by neighbors seeking security or some form of effective governance via collaboration with ISIL. A 2014 survey of over 4,000 displaced persons in northern Iraq conducted by the Nineveh Center for Research and Development revealed only 56% of respondents preferred to return to their homes. Approximately 42% preferred to migrate to another country.

Complicating matters further is that prior to ISIL's invasion, in accordance with the provision of the Iraqi Constitution that affords ethno-religious minorities the right to administer their own affairs, the Iraqi Government endorsed a proposal for the creation of the Nineveh Plains Governorate. The Plains Governorate would be split from the larger Nineveh Governorate and tied to Baghdad. This post-ISIL solution is consistently referenced as desirable in discussions with displaced persons wishing to return to Nineveh and members of the Assyrian and Yezidi diaspora communities appealing to the U.S. Government for aid.

The creation of a safe-haven without a proper administrative mandate for governance, security, population reconciliation, and a timetable for either long-term preservation or integration into Iraq makes the realization of the Nineveh Plains Governorate all the more difficult. The concern being as long as the safe-haven is present a Nineveh Plains Governorate is not. Again, preferential treatment of minorities via a safe-haven may stoke resentment from other groups. The same minorities that greeted news of a Nineveh Plains Governorate with outright or cautious optimism before ISIL would have their sense of security further decrease while their political and cultural isolation from the rest of Iraq's majority Arab and Muslim population increase. This would be a difficult blow to endure considering many minorities that favored the creation of a new governorate attached to Baghdad felt such an act demonstrated their loyalty to the Iraqi state and an ethnically inclusive Iraqi national identity. And that is to say nothing of the violence and oppression such groups have experienced over the last fifteen years.

Land Grabs and Loyalty Pledges

As the Iraqi Army retreated in summer 2014 and Baghdad dithered and crumbled, the KRG saw an opportunity to beat back ISIL and (re)claim territory it saw as rightly theirs. One possible future scenario has the Kurds using these land seizures against Baghdad 1) when and if final negotiations over the disputed territories or Kurdish independence take place; or 2) the economic and political fissure between Erbil and Baghdad worsens. Perhaps the more plausible scenario is the Kurds have no intention of ever relinquishing this territory. The Kurdish Declaration of Allegiance many displaced persons of northern Iraq are being presented with appears to signal as much. The Declaration of Allegiance has four main points signatories must sign "on their own volition with no pressure or coercion:"

- We stand unified with the President of Kurdistan, Mr. Masoud Barazani, and the heroes of the Peshmarga troops, and in support of them against terrorism and against any looming threats to the security and safety of the territory of Kurdistan.
- We ask the President, Mr. Masoud Barazani, to supervise the operation of

75

liberating Nineveh in collaboration with the Iraqi Army, and the "People (Popular) Troops" (from Nineveh) and to assure the lawful conditions during and after the liberation.

- We declare our support to return the annexed regions from Kurdistan back to Kurdistan. We also declare our full support to the right of Kurdistan to decide its fate to include its right to declare an independent Kurdish state.
- We support the creation of National Nineveh District, with its capital the City of Mosul in a strategic unity with the territory of Kurdistan, and to expedite the establishment of a transition committee for the territory of Kurdistan.

Calls for a safe-haven are a noble effort that increases awareness to ISIL's horrors. But those concerned with the plight of minorities in Iraq should redirect their focus from a plan with little chance of implementation or success to a more long-term solution. That is, 1) the return to the Nineveh Plains those displaced persons that wish to do so; 2) the initiation of efforts at inter-group reconciliation; 3) the implementation of the 2014 Nineveh Plains Governorate proposal and with it negotiations over disputed territories; and 4) the establishment of effective governance therein, including the integration of the governorate into a federal Iraq. This is indeed a tall order. But if Iraq is to succeed as a stable nation-state with a diverse ethno-religious population, ethnic particularism, no matter how well intentioned and how mild the form, is not the answer.

MATERIAL SUBMITTED FOR THE RECORD BY THE HONORABLE CHRISTOPHER H. SMITH, A REPRESENTATIVE IN CONGRESS FROM THE STATE OF NEW JERSEY, AND CHAIRMAN, SUBCOMMITTEE ON AFRICA, GLOBAL HEALTH, GLOBAL HUMAN RIGHTS, AND INTERNATIONAL ORGANIZATIONS

CUA

THE CATHOLIC UNIVERSITY OF AMERICA
Columbus School of Law
Interdisciplinary Program in Law & Religion
Washington, DC 20064

Robert A. Destro, Director
Direct Dial: 202-319-5202

DOCUMENTING THE GENOCIDE, WAR CRIMES & CRIMES AGAINST HUMANITY BY ISIL AND AFFILIATES AGAINST

CHRISTIANS, YEZIDIS, SHIA MUSLIMS & OTHER RELIGIOUS & ETHNIC MINORITIES

A WHITE PAPER

By
Robert A. Destro
(robertdestro@outlook.com)
Carole O'Leary, Ph. D
(carole.oleary01@gmail.com)
Richard C Michael
(rich1151@me.com)

May 25, 2016

Documenting Genocide, War Crimes & Crimes Against Humanity
by ISIL and Affiliates
against Christians, Yezidis, Shia Muslims & Other Religious & Ethnic Minorities

Overview

No subject better encapsulates the challenges facing American policy in the Middle East than the situation of the millions of refugees and internally displaced persons (IDPs)[1] who have been uprooted by war, sectarian violence and genocide[2] in Iraq and Syria. Among these challenges are:

- Defeat of ISIL and liberation of occupied communities;
- Pacification and stabilization of liberated communities;
- Providing material support and security for refugees and IDPs in diaspora;
- Representation of minority religious and ethnic communities in peace talks;
- Return of refugees and IDPs to their communities of origin;
- Creation of "safe havens" for minority religious and ethnic communities;
- Political and economic stabilization of post-war communities;
- Asylum and immigration policies for refugees and IDPs who want to leave; and
- Prevention and punishment of the genocide, war crimes and crimes against humanity committed by ISIL and its affiliated organizations in the Middle East and North Africa[3].

This White Paper argues that none of these problems can be addressed adequately without access to accurate, detailed information about these communities prior to and after their persecution and displacement. Policy makers and planners at every level need to have access to robust information about the demographics of these communities; their religious beliefs, social, and cultural characteristics; their political attitudes and loyalties; and some sense of the human capital resources on which they will rely as they seek to rebuild their lives and communities.

---

[1] By any measure, the numbers are staggering:

Country of origin	Refugees	IDPs (estimated)
Syria	4,844,111	864,609[1]
Iraq	377,747[1]	3,350,000[1]

Sources: UN High Commissioner for Refugees (UNHCR), *Syria IDP Operations. 2016*, 17 May 2016, available at: http://www.refworld.org/docid/573eac464.htm [accessed 22 May 2016]; Source: Internal Displacement Monitoring Centre at: http://www.internal-displacement.org/middle-east-and-north-africa/iraq/ (accessed May 22, 2016); UN High Commissioner for Refugees (UNHCR), Iraq: CCCM Settlement Status Map (30 April 2016), 30 April 2016, available at: http://www.refworld.org/docid/5732d9d54.html [accessed 22 May 2016]

[2] On March 17, 2016, Secretary of State, John Kerry, declared "that, in my judgment, Daesh is responsible for genocide against groups in areas under its control, including Yezidis, Christians, and Shia Muslims." John Kerry, Secretary of State, *Remarks on Daesh and Genocide*, March 17, 2016 at: http://www.state.gov/secretary/remarks/2016/03/254782.htm (accessed May 22, 2016).

[3] On March 10, 2016, the United States House of Representatives adopted House Concurrent Resolution 75 by a vote of 393-0. The Resolution expresses the sense of Congress that ISIL is committing genocide, war crimes, and crimes against humanity against Yezidis, Christians, Shia Muslims and other religious minorities. On April 28, 2016, the Senate Foreign Relations Committee reported the Senate version of the genocide resolution, Senate Resolution 340. At this writing, it is pending on the Senate calendar.

Documenting Genocide, War Crimes & Crimes Against Humanity by ISIL and Affiliates against Christians, Yezidis, Shia Muslims & Other Religious & Ethnic Minorities

Mapping Waves of Refugees

Today's refugee/IDP crisis in the northern governorates of Iraq, in Syria, in southern Turkey, and in Lebanon, Jordan and elsewhere is the inevitable result of violence against, and forced migration of generations of ethnic and religious groups in the region in the region. The long-suffering minority peoples of the region have experienced large, crippling waves of forced migration since at least the 1970s under the Arab nationalist (Baathist) governments of Syria and Iraq. The mass migrations of minority communities that occurred during and after both World War I and World War II are part of the same dismal pattern.

A recurring theme in these horrific accounts of human suffering is that singular, violent events perpetrated by terrorists (or rulers acting like terrorists) against minorities trigger mass migrations that decimate minority communities over wide areas.

A good example of the cumulative effect of rapid out-migration as a result of sectarian violence can be seen in the decline in the Christian population of Iraq from 1.4 million in the 1987 census to, perhaps, as few as 150,000 today. (Similar data is not available for the Yazidi community.)

Mapping and analyzing both the mass migrations triggered by these events, and developing robust survey data on the migrant communities is critical if policy-makers and planners are to understand the key issues, including the willingness of refugees and IDPs to return to their communities-of-origin and the contours of programs designed to reintegrate them into the sometimes-hostile majority populations from which they came. Documentation of atrocities, including crimes against humanity, war crimes and genocide, will also require significant documentation, including the identification of witnesses and victims; collection of statements from those having knowledge of specific crimes; identifying the actors who committed these crimes; graves registration; gathering and preservation of forensic evidence; and documentation of the destruction of cultural treasures – just to name a few

A detailed study of Christian IDPs in Ainkawa conducted by the authors in 2011/2012 (http://www.mena-rf.org/maps-downloads.html), found that most IDP waves correlated with specific acts of AQ/AQI terror, most notably the bombing of 5 churches in Mosul and Baghdad on 1 August, 2004, kidnappings of high-profile priests and church officials in the Nineveh Plain during 2006 and 2007, and the bombing of the Sayidat al-Neja Church in Baghdad during high Mass on Sunday, 31 October, 2010. Mass migrations of minorities also followed the Islamic State's (ISIL's) high-profile and well-publicized barbaric slaughter (and enslavement) of Shia Muslims, Yezidis, and others. The situation in Syria is more complex, but we are confident that surveys will show that specific, deliberate acts of terrorism (ISIL and state-sponsored) and religious and ethnic persecution have played a major role in driving minorities from their communities.

Goals

1. To achieve more accurate understandings of the situational context in which these religious communities find themselves, through gathering and analysis of robust data concerning the social, cultural, political, security, economic, and psychological factors affecting these communities; and

2. To link our analysis of these refugee and IDP communities to an analysis of the current security environment in the Kurdistan Region and Northern Syria, including identification of potential threats and challenges in this security context.

Documenting Genocide, War Crimes & Crimes Against Humanity
by ISIL and Affiliates
against Christians, Yezidis, Shia Muslims & Other Religious & Ethnic Minorities

Deliverables

Data collection: Expanding and collating existing databases containing information on the post-June 2014 IDP and refugee communities now living in the Kurdistan Region of Iraq (KRI) under the protection of the Kurdistan Regional Government (KRG). Existing rapid GIS-based cultural mapping/survey methodology developed for rapid data collection in conflict zones (or emerging/declining conflict zones) will be employed.

Data analysis: Once the data is collected and collated, it will be analyzed with a view toward gaining a better understanding of the social, cultural, religious, political and economic context in which the IDPs and refugees are living. This information is mission-critical not only for the IDPs and refugees themselves, who need a better understanding of their own communities' aspirations for their future, but also national and international security, redevelopment and relocation agencies.

At present, little accurate information is known about the locations that IDPs and refugees see as their ultimate destinations. Some will undoubtedly wish to remain in Ainkawa and the Kurdistan Region, where Archbishop Warda is expanding the infrastructure needed to support education, counseling and health care; others will want to return to their homes in the Nineweh Plain, or to join relatives outside of Iraq in the MENA region; and some will want to emigrate to Europe, the Americas or Australia. Even less is known about the human resources available in these communities, or about the political forces shaping their attitudes about the future.

Data Collection:

1) **Statistically valid surveys of current refugees and IDPs in Iraqi Kurdistan, Turkey and, if feasible, northeastern Syria.**

Surveys should focus on determining population statistics and demographics of the refugee/IDP communities, and capture detailed information about their places of origin, dates and reasons for leaving, gather preliminary evidence of violence against individuals and communities, and gather existing data about the destruction of cultural artifacts and religious sites that will assist those who will investigate their destruction. The survey activity should include a fully developed, legally-sound questionnaire, and the sampling framework must comply with rigorous, generally-acceptable statistical standards.

The research we propose would build on demographic, humanitarian and minority surveys we have undertaken in Northern Iraq between 2000 and 2012. The last phase of this work (2011-2012) established detailed demographic, religious, humanitarian profiles of the indigenous Christian communities of Iraqi Kurdistan. Previous work (still largely restricted) looked at the diverse populations of Kirkuk, Nineweh and the three KRG governorates of Erbil, Suliemania and Dohuk, with a particular focus on Kurds and IDPs. Those geographically-oriented surveys should be updated and expanded to include Christian, Yazidi, Shabaks, Kaka'is, Shi'a and other religious minorities who entered the KRI as IDPs after ISIS took Mosul in June 2014. Were adequate funding available, the research should be expanded to include IDPs and refugees in Nineweh and Kirkuk governorates as well as in Syria, Turkey, Jordan, Lebanon and Europe.

Documenting Genocide, War Crimes & Crimes Against Humanity
by ISIL and Affiliates
against Christians, Yezidis, Shia Muslims & Other Religious & Ethnic Minorities

2) **"Atmospheric" surveys of displaced minorities in Iraqi Kurdistan, Turkey and, if possible, northeastern Syria**

Attitude surveys of the refugees and IDPs will also provide critical information that will enable policy and development planners to anticipate the reactions in these communities towards programs designed to return them to their homes. Robust, reliable information is needed concerning refugee and IDP attitudes towards other populations inhabiting the areas from which they were forced, their political allegiances (if any), and other "human environment" factors that affect the long-term viability of re-settlement and re-integration programs.

3) **Historic population baselines for Christians, Yazidis, Shabaks, Kaka'is and other religious and ethnic minorities in Iraq and Syria.**

Because this information is not readily available, the information would be compiled and extrapolated from existing data, including:

a. *Census data is available for 1957 and 1987 in Iraq. Syria may have more recent census data.* We recognize that the Arab nationalist mandate of the Baath Party in Syria and Iraq did not recognize "ethnicity" (*e.g.*, Kurds, Assyrians, Turkomans, etc.), but they did record religious minorities in their census data. By using census data, we can identify definitively communities that were historically Christian, Yazidi, or other minority faiths; understand their historical size and make up; establish historic household demographics (age, size and sex) to determine the natural growth rate of Christian, Yazidi and other populations; and determine whether specific communities were gaining or losing population prior to the onset of conflict and ISIL.

b. *Parish, church, mosque and temple records, where available,* would help planners to better understand migration/IDP/refugee issues as well as to update, supplement or correct census data. We recommend analyzing parish records from 2003 to present.

c. Analysis of available data from the United Nations, World Bank, Food and Agriculture Organization, and NGOs working in the region.

d. Review of information on the web and other public sources

Examples of Deliverables

1) An initial compilation of existing information on religious minority communities from public and private sources;

2) Documentation and maps of cultural and religious communities before and after June 2014 in selected areas of Iraq and Syria;

3) Defensible historic Christian, Yazidi and other minority populations and their demographic baselines in Iraq and Syria based on the sources listed above;

4) Documentation and maps of significant religious sites and treasures prior to June 2014 (this information would necessarily be limited to more prominent sites given budget and financial restraints);

5) A fully developed, legally sound questionnaire that explores demographics; displacement; violence against individuals and communities; and destruction cultural and religious sites;

6) Preliminary documentation of alleged war crimes, crimes against humanity, and genocide, and collation of existing databases created by NGOs and other organizations in the region;

Documenting Genocide, War Crimes & Crimes Against Humanity
by ISIL and Affiliates
against Christians, Yezidis, Shia Muslims & Other Religious & Ethnic Minorities

7) Project database;
8) A user-friendly and informative interactive website;
9) Map of cultural and religious communities before June 2014;
10) Christian, Yazidi and other minority population and demographic baselines for Iraq and Syria based on the sources listed above;
11) Map of cultural and religious sites and treasures prior to June 2014;
12) Imaging and translation of key documents.

www.ingramcontent.com/pod-product-compliance
Lightning Source LLC
Chambersburg PA
CBHW081846280526
45789CB00007B/2585